You++

How to be More

Successful by

Embracing

AI

JOHN MICHAELIS

You++

First published in 2020 by

Panoma Press Ltd
48 St Vincent Drive, St Albans, Herts, AL1 5SJ, UK
info@panomapress.com
www.panomapress.com

Book layout by Neil Coe.

978-1-784529-19-2

The right of John Michaelis to be identified as the author of this work has been asserted in accordance with sections 77 and 78 of the Copyright, Designs and Patents Act 1988.

A CIP catalogue record for this book is available from the British Library.

This book is available online and in bookstores.

ACKNOWLEDGEMENTS

As I wrote this book, I thought about so many of the people I have had the pleasure to meet, work and socialise with over the course of my life. They are too numerous to mention. I am humbled that I am now an 'author.' I feel that in reaching this milestone I am 'standing on the shoulders of giants.'

My journey with AI has been long. I greatly appreciate the support of family and friends; they know who they are. I acknowledge by name the specific people who have been, and still are, with me in my day-to-day work with AI. The list is in alphabetical order.

Sam Abrika

Adam Benzecrit

Rafael Bloom

Barbara Bray

Anthony (Tosh) Brown

Hugh Carr-Archer

Josh Dykes

Maria de Fátima Marques

Amali De Silva-Mitchell

Mindy Gibbins-Klein

Simon Halberstam

Dr Tom Heseltine

Gary James

Sherin Mohamadali

Helen Prentice

Lee Scorer

Dr Przemyslaw (Shamek) Szeptycki

Blaise Thomson

Matt Urhammer

Patrick Usher

Professor Michel Valstar

Geoff Wainwright

Dr Nick Whitehead

Ayomiku Williams

Josh Wood

CONTENTS

INTRODUCTION

In 2014 the public became more aware of Artificial Intelligence (AI). Notable people, such as Professor Nick Bostrom, Professor Stephen Hawking and Bill Gates, predicted that AI would take over humans.

As we enter the 2020s there is general acceptance that AI does not pose such a threat. However, what is clear is that it will transform life as we know it. So much so that it has been termed 'the fourth industrial revolution'.

AI is a component of many beneficial products and services we use daily, but its effect is already being felt in the job market. For example, Microsoft recently announced that it would replace contract journalists on its MSN website and use automated systems, powered by AI, to curate articles.

I am fortunate to have been at the leading edge of the practical use of AI for over a decade. I can attest to how it can transform customers' experiences. I also have the learnings from many projects that never made it to market!

AI is available to individuals, small businesses and large businesses; using it does not require technical expertise. I believe that, as with any transformation, there will be winners and losers. I think the winners will be those who embrace AI and use it to augment their personal attributes and skills.

I hope this book can help you be a winner. It is written for ambitious people who wish to do their job better, pursue a personal passion for monetary reward or personal fulfilment, or just use their lives more productively.

I hope to inspire you to consider how you can use AI to pursue a successful business venture, get noticed at work, get more from your hobbies and pastimes, and feel more fulfilled. I recognise that many readers will have concerns that AI will take their jobs. Undoubtedly some will go but I believe that more will be created. I hope that once you have read this book you will be better placed to realise these opportunities.

This guide comprises nine chapters that are segmented into four parts.

Part 1 (Chapters 1 and 2)

Discusses the current state of play with AI, where it is used, how you may have experienced it and the unique capabilities you have which AI can't replace.

Part 2 (Chapters 3, 4 and 5)

This covers what I think you need to know to be able to work with AI. This includes how you get started with it as well as information and examples about what AI does, how you can reap the benefits and be less likely to succumb to unhelpful use cases.

Part 3 (Chapters 6, 7 and 8)

Provides a detailed discussion about types of roles you currently see in the workplace and how they may change.

Additionally, there is a framework for you to use if you wish to develop your own business or side hustle. As well as work and business examples, I outline creative and sporting endeavours that use AI.

Part 4 (Chapter 9)

This section provides some ideas on how routines may change over the next few years and how you may use AI in your daily life.

The book is written in an easy style, to both provide insight and stimulate ideas.

I sincerely hope you can use it to better yourself and realise some of your dreams.

It's always good to talk; please don't hesitate to connect with me.

Email: john@collaborative-ai.com

LinkedIn: https://www.linkedin.com/in/john-michaelis/

Twitter: JohnMichaelis@JohnMichaelis10

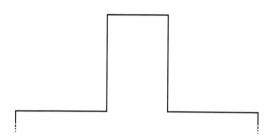

PART 1

THE
CURRENT
YOU

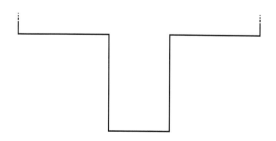

CHAPTER 1:

AI is Changing the Way We Live

They know what we want!

AI touches so much of our lives today, and we may not even realise it. Being online is an integral part of our everyday lives. Whenever we are online, we leave a comprehensive data trail that the global technology companies, the FAANGs (Facebook, Apple, Amazon, Netflix and Google) use to help them market to us services we may be interested in.

For example: yesterday I viewed some home furnishing sites as I'm refurbishing my office; today, when I view Facebook or Google, I find adverts inserted into my browser for office lighting and desks. I look on Amazon to see what they have to offer, the first page presented to me suggests toys I may be interested to purchase for my grandson. In the evening I go on to Netflix and am offered films that I may like. It is now common for AI to be used to predict what we may wish to buy.

The simple scenario I painted does not do justice to the scale of data gathering and sophistication of the AI computations. The data gathered covers far more than just items I have shown interest in previously; it includes more details from my browsing history, such as the sites I viewed prior to looking at the home refurbishing sites, sites I went to afterwards, anything I have asked of Google assistant or Alexa, my location, patterns of journeys made during the week, other publicly available data about me, and so it goes on.

Companies are continuously building a profile of us all, for their own marketing purposes. They assess typical and future behaviours associated with our profile and then use this to identify products and services to market to us. Other companies may make use of some of this data to assess our match to a recruitment specification, recommend people to meet for a date, assess our suitability for credit and our level of risk for insurance purposes.

I am not a keen shopper; I probably make unplanned purchases once every 6–8 weeks based on these proactive, targeted adverts. They are usually purchases driven by emotion or curiosity: toys for my grandson, books or events that cover topics that I may not realise are of interest to me, but suddenly spark my curiosity. I find it really spooky that AI can predict what I want to buy before I realise it!

Sometimes I have been upsold. For example, last year I was looking for dining room chandeliers. Using Google search, I found some suppliers of suitable products. I browsed through the sites and revisited them several times over the subsequent few weeks. I started to find adverts from lighting companies in my Facebook feed; I clicked on one online supplier who was quite upmarket and looked at their website a few times. I then started to see adverts from a manufacturer of bespoke chandeliers, who was located within reasonable travelling distance from my home. These adverts were persistent, and it was in fact this firm that I finally bought the chandeliers from. As the chandeliers were made especially for me, I probably paid double the price of buying a high-class standard piece from one of the top-end lighting retailers.

The power of AI is that it can look beyond what we say we want to do; I did not think for one minute I was going to buy two bespoke chandeliers. The details collected about us are used to create a profile. These are then matched against millions of other profiles, behaviour traits are analysed, and predictions are made about what we may really want. This isn't a perfect science; humans are emotional and illogical, so the AI isn't always right. We probably do not notice the times it gets it wrong as we will not pay attention to adverts that aren't relevant to us. When we spend no time dwelling on an advert, the AI will quickly compute that we aren't interested in that particular item.

How effective is this marketing? It is probably a little hit and miss but as the systems use AI they learn from our responses to adverts and information presented to us. This learning capability is what differentiates AI from previous technologies. The more data AI receives, the more it learns; the more it learns, the better it gets. It is this learning that makes AI so powerful as a profiling tool.

There may be an argument that AI isn't really offering any greater skill than a smart marketeer. You could argue that all AI is doing is the sort of analysis that a marketeer would do anyway. Looking at preferences expressed by prospective customers and then assessing their reaction to various promotions. This argument does have merit, apart from (i) AI is doing this rapidly on an industrial scale, which wouldn't be possible through human action and (ii) the AI computations are based on so much data that no human could extract all the trend information from that data and use it to predict future behaviour so accurately.

Certainly, in projects I have been involved in, we find that AI machine learning can extract information from data that no human can see.

As well as prediction, AI is helping us in many other ways:

It listens to us

Another aspect of AI that may touch your daily life is the use of AI for speech recognition. You may ask Google Assistant, Siri or Alexa to play music for you, tell you what is in your diary or call one of your contacts. The listening skills of these tools have been honed over the last decade by the use of speech-to-text and text-to-speech technologies. You may remember the acute frustration trying to use personal assistants a few years ago. You needed to speak with them in a quiet space and then the accuracy was poor.

People love talking; you may be one of the many who prefer to speak rather than type. There has been, and continues to be, significant investment in perfecting speech recognition.

Currently, most industrial systems are still only reliable for menu-driven requests. The most usable ones prompt the user for the answers they require; for example, a bank system may ask: "Please tell me what you want to do today — account balance, transfer money, pay bill, speak to agent". McDonald's is taking this a step further: it purchased a leading speech recognition company in 2019 and is using their technology to automate its drive-through ordering system to eliminate human operators. The technology is proven to be effective in noisy environments, offers a multilingual capability and is supposedly particularly good at recognising words, even from people with different accents.

Amazon Alexa and Google Home are the market-leading home-based personal assistants. Apple's Siri and Microsoft's Cortana are frequently used on phones and personal computers or tablets. However, I think it is fair to say that none of them understand the context and nuance of the spoken word. They do disguise this to some extent, as they can provide responses to open questions. They operate by identifying key words in a spoken sentence and playing something similar back to you. For example, if you ask Alexa to play a specific tune it repeats back to you the name of the tune it is going to play. This isn't because they are programmed to recognise specific words, but because they recognise sentence structure and can identify and extract the key word or words that they are looking for. They then match this key word or words to the tune you wish to hear or a specific task you want them to do.

All of these tools aid productivity by reading and setting calendar appointments, calling contacts, collating reminders and providing access to various applications where basic instructions are sufficient. Alexa and Google Home are also used for routine tasks such as controlling the central heating, playing music from Spotify or other music streaming applications, accessing home security cameras and systems, etc. Again, these are all tasks that you request by using specific words that AI can be trained to recognise. You need to be careful to use the name of the specific device you want to operate though.

Amazon runs a programme to encourage developers to produce tools based on Alexa, ie with Alexa as the core enabling technology. These are available through an online store under the Alexa Skills brand. You can think of these as similar to apps for your phone. In 2020 there were 70,000 Skills available in the Alexa store. This compares to about 2 million apps in the Apple app store and 2.5 million apps in the Google Play store. You may conclude that there are many unexploited opportunities to use Alexa; I think you would be right!

There is also a business program so organisations can develop capabilities based on Alexa. A high profile project is the automated butler that was deployed by Marriott in some of its hotels. The 'automated butler' replaces the need to call reception for room service or more toiletries; the customer just needs to speak their request to Alexa and the service is ordered. Alexa also acts as a concierge and books local restaurants and services.

Other businesses, such as Capital One, use Alexa for routine customer service enquiries such as checking account balances, spending trends and payment dates.

On the face of it there is considerable opportunity for wider use of Alexa, or similar capabilities, in society. However, the enthusiasm is dulled by concerns over privacy. Every request to Alexa is recorded and stored as an item of information; there have been examples of data privacy requests that have yielded a lengthy list of information that was gleaned by Alexa. The uncertainty in people's minds pertains to what else Alexa listens to and records. Does it really only record when someone says 'Alexa…'?

It knows who you are

There is so much electronic data about us nowadays, it is actually quite scary thinking about it. Do you use your face or your fingerprint to log into your mobile phone? Maybe you use your voice to gain access to your bank account? If you work on a major construction site, it's almost inevitable that the time and attendance system will require you to be recognised by a camera running face recognition or your palm print. Just reflect – all these uses of our personal biometric features are things we have volunteered to use. We haven't done anything wrong and been added to a database of miscreants.

Air travel takes this 'voluntary enrolment' a step further towards compulsion. Airports are using automatic face recognition to match travellers' faces to the pictures on their passports. Applications are predominantly for immigration, letting people back into their country of origin or where there are no entry restrictions.

Heathrow airport in London, UK is leading the way in using facial biometrics and AI to automate the whole passenger journey and improve the passenger experience. This includes the critical activities from a security standpoint such as passenger boarding. At the time of writing, the largest global implementation of automated passenger boarding and transit through the airport is being implemented. As well as checking the traveller's face against their passport, a biometric facial image is captured and aligned to the traveller's boarding pass as they enter the airside area. This means that the boarding pass, the traveller and their passport are all matched.

AI is enabling other aspects of the passenger journey too. Heathrow boasts that in the future it will be unnecessary to remove liquids from baggage: AI is being used to augment numerous security applications, to process images, align baggage to travellers and even profile travellers, thus ensuring safety levels are retained but passenger throughput and convenience can be increased.

If you cheat the system it will find you

For many years profiling and contact mapping have been important tools in the fight against organised crime and money laundering. AI enables these processes to be undertaken on an industrial scale. It also spots trends that humans and ordinary computation will miss. For example, a recent trend in money laundering has been for the bad actors to open multiple bank accounts and pass modest sums through each that are below the level which banks will investigate. Developing and matching profiles helps to spot aliases and these sorts of activities. The reader may be more familiar with the way their smartphone or computer occasionally alerts them to contacts that seem to be the same and asks if you want to merge them. Think of the anti-money laundering and security applications as being like this on a grand scale.

There are other industries that need to identify problematic actors. The online gaming industry has been pressured through commercial imperatives and regulatory fines to identify profiles associated with problem gamblers, both those who can outwit the bookies and people with gambling addictions. Over the last two years, many of the household name companies in the industry have turned to AI to help them identify these profiles, including when it is a single actor with multiple aliases.

There is a feeling that some of the social media companies have been slow to spot fake accounts and malevolent content. Facebook initially relied on user advice to identify issues. When this proved insufficient, they hired teams of reviewers; however, these did not scale sufficiently. Over the last two or three years they have developed AI tools to examine content, especially images, to detect material that should not be online.

Earlier this year (2020), Facebook announced that it was using an AI-based system it calls Deep Entity Classification (DEC) and had already taken down millions of fake accounts. The DEC system does not just analyse the individual account, it also looks at how it interacts with other accounts and pages. This means that potentially thousands of data items are used to make the decision whether an account is legitimate or not. Such analysis would not be possible using human review or traditional computing techniques.

Robots do the hard work

Japan led the world in automating factory lines during the 1970s and 1980s while the manufacturing sector in the UK was burdened through overmanning and lack of investment. This led to industrial unrest and a lack of competitiveness from both a cost and quality standpoint.

Japan was focussed on design excellence, streamlined processes and automation of repetitive tasks.

Even though these early robots were purely automating specific manual processes and had no intelligence, the superior productivity of the Japanese approach highlighted the weaknesses associated with a human workforce. People are unable to work consistently 24/7 and they sometimes make mistakes or do things slightly differently, even when the actions for a required task are exactly the same.

At first these machines required precision setup for a single specific job or to be specifically programmed. Now that artificial intelligence can be used to program these robotic machines, they are able to read designs, for example from CAD, and adapt their movements accordingly. AI also aids quality control. Cameras can see items in more detail than the human eye and AI programs can be trained to recognise defects that would be indiscernible to people.

AI enables the use of robots that move around too. It is the key to the intelligence that driverless cars will need. In the meantime, we see robots being used in warehouses. However, these robots are still mostly controlled by preset programs or manual guidance. Amazon is testing robots that have sufficient intelligence to pick items off the shelves, but still believes that the unmanned warehouse is a long way off. I do see significant advances being made in domestic robots, especially those for home cleaning like vacuuming. There are numerous models on the market that can learn the best route round the house and identify obstacles. Additionally, they are equipped to respond to voice commands; some models use Alexa technology for this.

You may even meet a robot in your local bank branch. HSBC deployed the Pepper robot from SoftBank into its flagship Manhattan branch and various other branches in US malls. The robot has a humanoid form. It greets customers when they enter the branch. Using speech recognition technology it can assist on ATM transactions and routine account queries as well as direct customers to the next available member of staff if their query is more complex. Pepper has been credited with increasing the overall volume of ATM transactions and credit card applications, as well as being well received by customers.

Just the start

AI has reached a point that I believe demonstrates its merit as a technology that will enable a quantum change in the way we do many things. I also feel that you, whoever you are and whatever you do, can be confident in finding ways that you can use the technology to augment your working and personal lives. We see already that AI is good for specific tasks, typically those that involve detailed processing of huge volumes of data or replacing routine tasks, but it still needs marshalling to the applications and usage models where it can add greater value.

CHAPTER 2:

You Have the Personal Attributes to Do Well with AI

"As more and more artificial intelligence is entering into the world, more and more emotional intelligence must enter into leadership.[1]" These aren't my words but those of Amit Ray, the Indian author and spiritual master. I believe they are so apt and sit at the core of my belief

---

1   Amit Ray, *Compassionate Artificial Intelligence*

that everyone can do well with artificial intelligence. It is social interaction and how we make each other feel that enables 'things to get done.' What makes humans so able is emotional intelligence and the ability to communicate, it isn't just an ability to think logically and undertake tasks.

Everybody is capable of social interaction

Some of us are introverted, some extroverted, and most somewhere in-between. Maybe it's worth reflecting a minute:

Who do I really trust and achieve things with regularly? A partner? Family members? Friends? Work colleagues? Learning colleagues? People at sports or other leisure/ social clubs?

You may have listed a number of people or even groups of people. Common interest may be part of what binds you to these people. However, I expect the list is long and varied enough to demonstrate that every reader is capable of social interaction and the vagaries that go with it.

Further analysis may well lead you to conclude that it isn't always 'logical' for you to get on well with these people. Sports teams often unify people with varying levels of education and socio-economic background. Everyone collaborates effectively as they have the emotional intelligence to form these bonds, even though there are little, if any, logical pointers as to why they should be able to communicate effectively.

We meet people throughout our daily lives. The barista who sells us a coffee and pastry on our way to work, the bus driver or transport operative who checks our ticket or gives us directions, the security guard or receptionist when we enter a building, and then a whole range of work colleagues and support staff when we are at work. Some people seem to enjoy the service they receive from these people, others find it a chore. Maybe those that offer something and treat the person as a human get a better experience?

During the day we may have more structured engagement with team members or meet customers or suppliers relevant to our work. We may also meet people in the firm who we wouldn't normally collaborate with, especially if we are on a 'focus group' or similar exercise. At the end of the working day or week we get to do our social activities; maybe we just spend time with family, or more probably with friends and meeting new people. Again, this may be in a structured environment such as a sports team or similar or less structured in a pub or other informal setting.

The point is that we are meeting all these people, using our social skills to make an impression and create an image of ourselves in their mind and also, maybe, to persuade them to do something. Most readers will already know that the words we hear from people makes up a small proportion of our overall impression of that person.

Emotional intelligence makes the world go round

I grew up in the 1960s. At that time, we still had the cold war. The public sector ran utility services, public transport and undertook some manufacturing; public sector workers were unionised. We had a society that operated on a 'command and control' model. Productivity was low and by the 1970s we faced the near collapse of the economy when a three-day working week was imposed. People didn't feel part of anything bigger that would make their lives better, so they just took entrenched positions.

It would seem that emotional intelligence was non-existent and we just had robot-like groups of people following the herd. However, if we look below the surface, we see numerous examples of how, by using their emotional intelligence and building human relationships, people did improve their lot.

At that time nearly half of the workforce was employed in blue collar roles in agriculture, manufacturing, ports, construction, and coal mining. Often they worked in a shift-based system, sometimes including overnight work.

Many of these workforces were unproductive. This was the cause of the steep decline in the UK's economic fortunes in the 1970s, which culminated in the rise of the services sector from the 1980s onwards. Let's take by way of example the shift-based workforce of the car manufacturers in the Midlands. The UK car industry at that time was persistently unproductive, which led to multiple rescue attempts by successive governments.

Was that just because the workers didn't work hard? No! The workers all had to clock on and clock off from work through a time and attendance machine. Management saw high attendance levels. What they didn't see was the co-operation between workers whereby they would agree to clock on their friends so they could have an extra day off. This wasn't a casual arrangement: groups agreed who would have which day of the week off, so the shop floor looked full to the managers and the 'escapees' weren't noticed.

This is a rudimentary example of how the emotional intelligence (of the workers) prevailed over the robotic command and control approach of management.

Turning the clock forward sixty years, say to 2030, will computers rule our lives as depicted in sci-fi movies such as *The Matrix*? I believe not. In a similar way to how people's emotional intelligence enabled them to collaborate and overcome the strictures of command and control I believe people will continue to control computers.

Many readers may be thinking, I am still not sure AI isn't going to rule my life. AI can be used to provide autonomous control to aggressive machines, such as military drones. It can be used for pervasive surveillance – an example is the use China makes of recognition and tracking systems to follow its citizens. In the West we willingly succumb to the influence of the technology by submitting information to social media and purchasing goods and services from the likes of Amazon and Netflix.

Of course, there will be international conventions and regulatory frameworks to prevent the technology being used for overall societal harm. Presuming most of the world adheres to them, these will be effective in some areas.

The reason I think that AI will not take over our lives is that it will be, what the citizens of the world consider to be reasonable use of the technology, that ultimately determines the acceptability and success of it. It will be the collective view of what people find acceptable and helpful, and how they cooperate to circumvent aspects they don't like, that will determine how successful applications are – again, emotional intelligence.

Evolution of self-awareness

We all have emotional intelligence. Over my lifetime I have witnessed society in general develop a greater awareness of what makes up emotional intelligence and how this knowledge can make for more influential and productive person-to-person engagements.

Many person-to-person engagements occur when one person is trying to persuade another to do something; a good example is persuading someone to buy something. Obviously, not everything we buy is proactively sold to us. We buy food, fuel and other necessities of life as we need to. Who we choose to buy them from, for example which shop, is a decision that is made based on logical factors such as quality, price, and convenience. Advertising by major brands tries to influence our perception of these attributes so that we are more likely to buy from their store. As this type of influence evolves, AI will undoubtedly have a role to play. That is discussed further on in this book.

The point here is that we all influence people, usually using our emotional intelligence. You have emotional intelligence built-in, so I don't believe you will be subordinated to a computer!

The evolution of persuasion is a lesson for the AI era

We all evolve and develop over time based on our environment and things that happen to us during life. I'll exemplify this by considering the evolution of professional sales techniques over the last 140 years.

The industrial revolution of the 1800s enabled the development of equipment for all types of work. One example was cash registers for use by shopkeepers. The National Cash Register (NCR) company is believed to have been a thought leader of the time when it came to professional sales techniques. Salespeople were taught to slavishly follow processes to identify and pursue opportunities. These included pre-scripted demonstrations and presentations of the equipment. While they had to establish a rapport with prospective customers, there was probably limited opportunity to really get to know them – emotional intelligence wasn't required to the same extent as we are used to nowadays.

Psychology was developing as a science at this time too. Wilhelm Wundt founded the Institute of Experimental Psychology in Germany. Sigmund Freud, the founder of psychoanalysis, postulated his theories about human behaviour.

It was in the 1930s that Dale Carnegie first wrote about the integration of psychology and process into the sales engagement. His most famous book is *How to Win Friends and Influence People*, which covered the skill of influence in general. He went on to author many books on sales skills and leadership. His work led the thinking on understanding the motivations of buyers and how the behaviour of the salespeople made them feel. His sales training techniques, especially a course called *Winning with Relationships*, are still popular today.

Over the remainder of the century, sales techniques became more sophisticated. Many of the learnings were used as part of the burgeoning leadership development industry, which had historically considered individual leadership traits rather than interaction with others.

As we entered the 1960s, there were technical advances in home appliances and equipment: double glazing, washing machines, televisions, etc all became more affordable. There were numerous outlets and organisations that needed to become adept at selling these products. They retained staff specifically for this purpose and trained them in the art of salesmanship. This involved being able to lead the customer through a decision-making process so they would place a purchase order at the time of the sales call. The process worked and was then extrapolated to other services including insurance and other financial arrangements. The difference between these processes and those of 70 years earlier was that the newer ones were far more interactive. Success was dependent on the salesperson's ability to pick up verbal and non-verbal clues from prospective customers and adjust their behaviour to help the customer feel good about making the purchase from them.

Good salespeople were typically ruthlessly driven, very resilient to rejection and developed an exceptional ability to rapidly establish a rapport with the customer and drive them through the decision-making process. The sales profession was never recognised as a true profession as there was a feeling that often salespeople were too pushy, and increasingly there were examples of sales people misrepresenting products.

Effective sales skills require well-developed emotional intelligence. Fact finding, understanding personality types, developing empathy and securing agreement from someone else have become common in society. People often display these without realising it.

As we enter the 21st century, the art of persuasion has taken on a more sophisticated form. In the previous chapter I outlined how the more advanced online sales companies use AI to predict what we may wish to purchase. There is also a wide range of information available on the internet so anybody can research what they are going to buy before they engage with a vendor. However, what is irreplaceable is the human ability to understand when, how and why someone would use an item or service they purchase.

Obtaining this information requires sensitive discussion and questioning, as well as a great deal of empathy. This can only be achieved by understanding how certain actions make people feel – a well-developed emotional intelligence.

Relevance to your use of AI

Where this is all heading is that the most successful users of AI will be those with the best developed emotional intelligence, as per the quote at the start of this chapter.

Everybody has emotional intelligence and can enhance it through a personal development process. Emotional intelligence has always been the way to get things done, and I think it will remain so for the foreseeable future and beyond.

AI is a tool and is found inside tools we can all use to improve our lives; ultimately, to use these tools effectively, it will be emotional intelligence that is required – and we all have it!

You are cleverer than you think

We have just discussed how our understanding and use of emotional intelligence has evolved over the last century or so. Before we get on to anything to do with AI let's consider at component level the subjective analysis we do for a large part of our day that contributes to our emotional intelligence. I believe that it is the human ability to read and contextualise multiple signals from other people that makes our emotional intelligence superior to anything AI will do in the foreseeable future.

- Body language – does the person lean forward and display interest, or do they move away from us? Do they cross their arms? Do they sit back and maybe slouch?

- Facial expression and head movement – sometimes people nod their head and smile when they agree; they look intently if they are interested or look away if they aren't. There is an old saying that if someone doesn't look you in the eye then they may not be being honest. If you are in a small audience (say less than 80 people) at a conference or similar event, try shaking your head when the speaker makes a few points – see what effect it has on them! If you think this is too cruel, try nodding your head, see how much they look at you!

- Pace and tone of speech – again, if someone speaks quickly, with little pausing we may assume they are nervous; if they speak more deliberately and calmly it gives the impression that they are the authority on the matter.

We take in all this information and form opinions on the situation dynamically. Just think about how much time you spend in a day meeting different people, all the signals you see every second and therefore how much information you process – amazing isn't it?

Now, let's look at how culture and modern life affect the signals we get and why our ability to contextualise a situation is so important. I'll share a couple of my faux pas!

I was doing business in Saudi Arabia about 10 years ago. I attended a meeting in Jeddah, which was less conservative than other parts of the country. Consequently, more women engaged in business. Typically, upon meeting, I would shake hands with the gentlemen but would not offer to shake hands with the ladies. I would stand slightly further back from them and respectfully say 'pleased to meet you' as I knew that many Saudi ladies preferred not to shake hands – even those in business. I got it spectacularly wrong in one meeting when the lady stepped slightly closer and stretched out her hand to shake hands, commenting that she expected to be treated as an equal with men!

I worked with an Indian company on a major IT consultancy project for the Kenyan Government. I was leading on the networking and communications pieces. As we went for the first meeting, I felt we were well organised and the five of us (four guys from the Indian company and I) were well coordinated. We took it in turns to explain the parts of the scope we were responsible for. I went through my piece and saw that some of the team were shaking their head. I found this disturbing but had to continue regardless. After the meeting they told me how pleased they were with the presentation. I asked about the head shaking, so they informed me that this is the way Indians show approval! Throughout the project when any of us shook or nodded their head we had to ask each other if it was an Indian or UK head shake!

Abstract thinking

One of the keys to influence is how you make people feel. There are people who build followings on YouTube, Instagram, Twitter, Facebook and LinkedIn. These may be for social purposes or business purposes; many relate to cultural activities. By projecting a persona or creating a movement, skilled operators can engender positive feelings, comfort or curiosity in their followers. However, I would argue that this appeals more to the human herd or tribe instinct rather than being the assimilation of information which I discussed above. Is it really different from the way people select a football team to follow and feel a sense of belonging from that?

What it does demonstrate is the importance of abstract thinking. The examples above show how people align to a concept, philosophy or a bunch of values. Putting these together and creating something that people can associate with is abstract thinking. We all see this in our day-to-day lives whenever there is an election. Politicians paint a picture of something better for us in the future without being specific about how it will be achieved and typically remaining thin on detail.

It isn't just politicians and leaders who use abstract thinking; we all do. It is something that computers can't do, and AI is unlikely to be able to do either. It forms the basis of our imagination, how we develop theories to explain observations, and also our ability to develop analogies to explain something complex in simple terms. Abstract thinking is a fundamental part of our emotional intelligence. It is what we use to understand how something we do may make people feel and helps us develop stories which are often a better way of explaining a point to people than using hard facts.

Think about the last time you saw a stand-up comedian. They often tell stories about real life situations we all experience, for example getting the children ready for school or getting stuck in a traffic jam. The comedian's ability is to take these standard situations and make them seem funny. The best ones are very skilful at using humour to establish an emotional connection with an audience.

Critical thinking

So far I have discussed emotional intelligence and how that gives us superiority over computerised systems, even intelligent ones running AI. We must not neglect the left side of our brain. This enables logical thinking. Everybody's level of intelligence and education differs; however, that doesn't mean that people can't interpret information and form opinions on whether it is true or not. This is critical thinking. Again, it is something AI can't readily replicate but people are very good at.

You may react intuitively to a claim to decide whether it is true or not; alternatively, you may seek hard evidence. We often use a mix of the two. Many public service providers obsess with providing statistics about the performance of their services, for example punctuality of a train service. If your regular commuter train has been late every day you may well question claims that the service is running well.

Everyone is capable of critical thinking – it is intuitive. Just think how many times you have heard someone ask, "So, how does that work, then?" or say, "I don't believe it, every time I attend... I have to wait an hour. Who only waits 15 minutes?"

There is no secret sauce

This chapter argues that everyone has the personal attributes to do well with AI. There are many things in life where a level of preparation and planning increase the chances of success. Using AI is no different.

Let's take a long car journey as an example. In the olden days I used to look at maps and write down my route before I set off. I would also note some alternatives in case one route was blocked. The advent of sat-nav systems eased this process, as they would recommend a route; however, it was typically best to use them as a supporting tool rather than the definitive guide. Nowadays we have Google Maps and Waze which dynamically assess the traffic on a route and update their guidance. Again, though, it is often best to have undertaken a level of pre-planning at least to assess the likely time the journey should take and decide how much contingency to add.

As we enter the AI era we will rely more and more on AI for routine tasks. It is how we link together routine tasks and analyse the information we receive that differentiates between success and failure; this will not change with AI. Developing a strategy and plans to execute these strategies will continue to be key to success.

You can use AI

Technical advances in the deployment of AI mean it is available for consumption on a subscription basis from the FAANGs and increasingly from others. You don't need to be a technical genius, you need to have sufficient technical wherewithal to use apps on a mobile phone and basic computer programs such as MS Office or G Suite.

Maybe you already use Google Home or Alexa. Maybe you use some of the applications that Alexa can do through its Alexa Skills store. As long as you can frame the problem you want to solve, the chances are you will find the answer.

One of the key uses individuals will make of AI is as a personal assistant – maybe to book restaurants and make travel arrangements. In the near future, it could be used to organise appointments. You could use it in your business. Suitable problems are: predicting an outcome based on previous behaviours, profiling customers to target offerings, estimating a future value, assessing customer sentiment or analysing images. The only skill you will need will be the ability to frame the problem and gather sample information.

The coronavirus pandemic focussed business minds on working remotely. What if you need to do more remote selling? There are tools available that tell you how customers react to your sales pitch so you can adapt it mid-flight to trigger a more agreeable response. I offer a few guidelines to be successful with AI. These are:

1. Develop your personal vision of what/who you want to be. This shouldn't be based on securing a position in your company or particular status in society, but based on your human strengths and values.

2. Look at your day-to-day life and see how much of it is routine, both inside and outside of work. Think about how much more you could do if this routine was streamlined through the use of tools (typically AI).

3. Having identified the extra time, you will have to consider how you can best use this on your journey to reach your personal vision. Consider your own emotional intelligence, other human capabilities and life experiences, and bring these to bear as much as possible.

4. As you progress towards your personal vision think about how much better that vision would be if you had more information available to you, in real time. What would this information be? Are there tools available to help you secure this information?

5. Take the above, commit a portion of every week or month to personal development and learning, and commit to the strategy to realise your fullest personal vision.

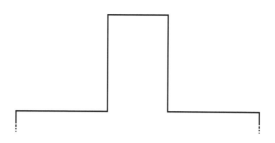

PART 2

WHAT YOU NEED TO KNOW

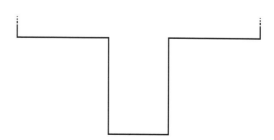

CHAPTER 3:

Think Ahead to be Successful in AI

Start dreaming

You may be asking yourself what do I want to do with AI? Think about your job, your hobbies, something you may wish to do as a side hustle. AI will give you the opportunity to transform how you do these things. Using AI will reduce time spent on routine and can help you target your efforts and be more productive. It also offers you the opportunity to develop unique insights that can enable you to develop your personal and/or professional profile and even earn more money.

AI is becoming available as a service, so you will not need to be an expert coder to use it. More and more, there are capabilities which require no coding expertise. There are services available with embedded AI that can enable text to speech conversion (and vice versa), personalise services and make product recommendations, assess sentiment, facilitate forecasting, and analyse text, video, images or audio.

The concept

AI is fundamentally different in the way it works to the legacy computing we are familiar with that processes information using formulas. An AI is created by teaching it using historic data. It then assesses new information, determines the level of certainty of an answer and reports that accordingly.

A classic example is that of the first AIs. These were shown pictures of an object or animal, for example a cat, and trained to recognise cats in pictures. You can find out more by typing 'Google cat research' into Google search. The AI was trained to recognise cats by being shown thousands of pictures of different cats in different environments and at different angles. Having been trained, the AI was shown a series of pictures, some containing cats and some not. The AI would then identify which pictures have cats in them. It may be that the AI is set to give a positive response if it is 75% certain there is a cat. The AI can then be trained further so that its level of certainty, and accuracy, increases. This is one of the wonderful things about AI, it gets better with use as long as it has a good teacher – YOU!

So what?

Then you may think, "What can I use it for?" The answer to that question lies in how you use information and/or engage with others. AI works well with unstructured data – this can be images, text, video, sound or any kind of data input. The difference is that AI isn't programmed, it is trained using historic data records and learns to do a task in the same way as humans. Therefore, as long as there is data to train the AI, it can rise to the challenge.

Examples of the problems AI can solve are:

- Estimate a Value

  AI can provide an estimated value that is unknown – for example, a journey time based on traffic volume, or a property price based on a textual description and address.

- Prediction

  This is often used to predict future buying behaviour based on a person's profile that typically includes records of previous purchases, internet searches and browsing history and other stated interests. There are numerous uses of this type of prediction based on profiling; some obvious ones are law enforcement, credit risk assessment, insurance risk assessment and health screening.

- Classification

  Classification problems include text and image analysis. For example, classifying news articles, eg whether they are about industry, domestic politics, international relations or sport (or none of the above). Other examples are (i) sentiment analysis – assigning a positive or negative sentiment to a paragraph of text reviewing a product or service, (ii) classifying the genre of a tune and (iii) classifying video streams using predetermined or customised labels.

- Detection

  This type of problem includes detecting a specific pattern within a block of information. This is particularly useful for text analysis where the AI develops an understanding of sentence structure and therefore can differentiate between types of names, ie it can determine if a name is a person, organisation or location without the use of look up lists.

- Comparison

  Given two items of data, return a quantified comparison according to some abstract criteria – such as indicating if two images of faces belong to the same person, or two paragraphs of text are written by the same author. This could be applied in determining plagiarism, for example.

Identifying your case(s) for using AI will require consideration. You need to think about how this problem-solving capability can help you and how you want to use it. I encourage you to think big and list down three to five ideas.

Let's get real

Once you have identified your initial ideas, think about how You, yes, your personal attributes, can use these solutions to best effect. Please remember Chapter 2: AI cannot replicate emotional intelligence, critical and abstract thinking, or creativity. Ask yourself what you do that utilises these capabilities.

Maybe you are in the hospitality sector or restaurant sector. Do your customers really value that attention from the waiter serving the food and drinks? Maybe they prefer to self-serve, perhaps from a conveyor belt of food with dishes on it like Yo Sushi? Maybe they would like to order from a terminal on their table and have the food delivered by a robot? Based on what customers order, you could use an AI recommendation engine to offer customers other items that compliment their selections. Despite the automation would customers still value knowing that there is someone 'owning' their experience? There could be customer experience staff ensuring that they are comfortable, content and feeling appreciated.

Perhaps you run a coaching or training business and are developing a range of online, on-demand offerings to complement the services you deliver personally. You could be raising your profile through blogging, providing some free content, or even hosting a YouTube channel. You will want your time to be spent securing customers and delivering the higher-value, more personalised services. You can use AI to better understand your customers and which services and content will most interest them. Amazon offers its Personalise programme, which enables businesses to use some of the Amazon AI profiling capabilities to create recommendations for customers.

These are just two examples of how AI could be applied. You could contemplate using it at work and suggest projects that could be beneficial. AI scales extremely well, reduces the burden of routine and provides insight before, during and after a customer engagement.

Enterprises seek to engage with their customers continuously. They use social media, have chatbots and call centres available and many still have retail or service delivery locations. These engagements generate a vast amount of data that can be used for a whole range of analyses. AI can also help streamline these engagements. For example, a travel company could use a chatbot for routine enquiries such as trip confirmations and payments and then divert more complex matters to staff at the call centre.

These are just a few examples, to give a flavour of the practical uses of AI. There are many, many more, some of which will be outlined in later chapters. These examples are here to help make an argument about planning ahead tangible for you.

Augment you

Once you are at a point where you have some ideas about how you can deploy AI, you can consider how you add massive value to the project by using human characteristics to provide a bespoke, empathetic customer experience.

You and other customer-facing people will be able to move up the value chain and spend time undertaking higher-value activities, leveraging their unique human strengths. The next thing to consider is how can AI augment these activities?

Think about what you are going to be doing: how will you be engaging with other people? Face-to-face? Video? Telephone? Will you be trying to encourage them to engage with you through advertising? Maybe by developing interesting or creative content?

Then think about what feedback or other information you would like as you engage. Are there tools available to help you glean that information? To help, I will provide an example.

Consider a telesales function. I am not thinking about people who cold call but about the sales desks at a bank, opening new bank accounts and selling credit cards, or a telecoms company where they want to sell more services – scenarios where the customer wants to buy, the question being how much can they be persuaded to buy.

Telesales agents speak on a phone based on prompts on their screen; typically the calls are not scripted so the agent needs to try and establish a rapport with the customer quickly based on the conversation. Most of us find this harder than in meetings where we can see peoples' facial expressions and body language.

Cogito Inc. provides a tool that gives sales and service agents insight into customer emotions during an engagement.

The Cogito system listens to the conversation and provides the agent with feedback on their behaviour and how the customer is feeling. The types of clues it looks for include levels of participation and energy, interruptions, tone and empathy. This information is provided in real time to agents so they can alter their approach dynamically to optimise their interaction.

Resource allocation is another challenge that AI can help with, especially staff rostering, which is a ubiquitous challenge for organisations. If this is something you do then you may already be using sophisticated models to do it. However, do they really use all of the relevant data to give the best option? The truth is, they don't, as there are more factors than the mind can compute which affect the demand for resources at a specific time. Instead of being bound by the data you can compute, think about all the parameters that may be relevant, get the data on them and then have the AI look for patterns and assist in the staff rostering.

Augmentation is one of the big opportunities to use AI. The question you should ask yourself is, "What information do I need to do my job much better?" Once you know that, you can seek commercially available tools to fulfil this need.

Data is key

This chapter is about thinking ahead to be successful with AI. At least as important as having a vision is having the data; in fact, understanding what data you have may actually inform the vision. If you have a vision then, ask yourself, "What data do I need to realise that vision?"

Do you really know how much data you acquire on a daily basis? If you run a retail business you probably know who buys what, how they pay and how often they buy. If you have an online presence you may hold more information about them. Where they live, what products and services they browsed before placing an order, maybe even how they found your site, and if you use the latest web tools you may also know from which website they arrived at yours and from and where they went to afterwards. You may even know how long they spent browsing on each page.

Data is the key to being successful with AI. Amazon and Google make no secret of the fact that first and foremost they are data acquisition companies and use this information to help promote products and services relevant to users.

Data can be in numerous formats. If you want to improve sporting team performance, then it may be videos of previous games. If you want to predict behaviour, then it is likely to be customer profiles. If you are engaged in a coaching, teaching or advisory capacity, then time to complete the answers could be a useful item to track in addition to responses to an assessment. Ideally, the data should be unique to what you want to achieve. If it isn't, then the question to ask is, "How can I add further value to the data?" Is it possible to combine it with other data, maybe some that is publicly available, to establish a unique data set that can be used to develop a valuable insight?

The next step in the thought process is to consider what data you can capture. Examples could be capturing video of someone engaging in an online course or capturing video of trainee actors and public speakers. This provides the raw data for analysis using biometrics and aspects of body language. In the medtech space there are companies like BlueSkeye that are already using face recognition technology to assess mental wellbeing. These applications are already being extended to assess levels of frustration and engagement. These could be valuable data items for a coach.

Now here is the part of the journey you may find more challenging: how to store the data and label it consistently so it can be used to train an AI program to do what you are wanting to do. This does sound frightening and it may be necessary to seek some help from someone with a college-level understanding of mathematics. Frankly, it is probably no harder than establishing a basic accounting process in a small business. There are tools becoming available that will take much of the grind out of this. These are available as cloud-based services, so there is no IT complexity to deal with.

The labelling is important, hence the need for someone who is used to working with data. Review the data you have and consider what insights you could glean from it. What can it tell you that you would find useful? As you answer this question, it is possible to work out what parameters you want to store and how you want the data labelled. Once you have done this, split the data into sub-sets for training the AI, validating it, further training and testing.

Now you have developed your ideas on how to extract value from the data, you can consider using the readily available AI tools from Google, Amazon and other global IT providers to glean the insights that will help your idea prosper.

What will they think?

You are probably concerned about your reputation. You may well wish to be seen as trustworthy, fair and respectful of others. You may have started to feel slightly anxious when you read about collecting and using personal data. It is important to be careful, like you are in many other situations. If you run a coaching business or are involved in financial services you probably hold much personal data. If you are an engineer you have to adhere to approved procedures every day to maintain safety. If you are in facilities management, IT or security you probably have access to much sensitive data. The point is that data management isn't new to us; we just need to be sensible.

AI does pose new challenges based on its predictive and classification capabilities. Anonymising the data you use for training the AI would be better, as long as you can demonstrate that individuals can't readily be identified from the anonymised data.

Alternatively, you can seek permission from the people whose data you are gathering to use it. This approach is often used by events companies and the marketing departments of large companies who may want to market various offerings to you. It is an approach used by many surgical teams to understand how effective their surgical procedure was, both in the immediate and longer terms.

Whichever approach you have to gleaning data, it is important that you use best practice to store and protect that data. Increasingly, data is being stored on cloud-based services from Amazon, Google and Microsoft as they provide a high level of assurance.

Am I being fair?

AI systems are trained on data. If that data isn't representative, then there is a chance that the AI system will be biased.

Recently, a leading US innovation and research institute, MIT (Massachusetts Institute for Technology) published a paper that outlined how a US Government research institute identified bias in most of the face recognition algorithms used in the US[2]. The study concluded that systems had a higher rate of false positive matches for Asian and African-American faces, the worst rates being for African-American women.

I expect that this is because most face recognition systems in the US have been developed for law enforcement and are trained on databases that have many more white and Hispanic males.

---

2   Karen Hao, MIT Technology Review, December 20, 2019

It is important that you are aware of the potential for unintended bias by AI systems. However, there are safeguards you can readily put in place to ensure that you continue to uphold your values.

The first thing is to assess how likely there is to be bias. There are a couple of basic things you can do:

1. Check the input data to see if there is potential for underlying bias. Just by looking at the data and perhaps doing some basic filtering on a spreadsheet, do you see a disproportionate proliferation of one data type?

2. When you test the AI you will use a specific data set for testing. Pay attention to this to ensure it provides a balanced representation of the community that will be analysed by the AI. Perhaps get it from different sources. You can then examine the output, not just for accuracy but also to see if the results may be reflecting some unintended bias based on any imbalances or trends you identified in the training data.

Even if you are concerned that the system may have some bias, I expect that you will still be able to use it. You will recall that AI works by statistical assessment of the probability of a match. Changing the threshold may reduce the accuracy of the system and could well reduce any bias tendencies. However, as most applications are either to support decisions made by humans or about running a business operation better, there is no real concern and no need to have a 100% accurate outcome. As they say, perfect is the enemy of good.

At the time of writing, the usual approach, for more critical decisions, is to add a human to the loop to check relevant aspects of the output and make the final decision. They can then check any particular information that may have been adversely affected by the bias and flag it so that future training of the AI takes it into account.

An example of this human in the loop approach is the operating model of the police forces in the UK when they use face recognition software to identify known criminals in a town centre. They will not stop anyone in the street until an officer has checked the images and verified it is the required miscreant.

I leave you with this summary message: you should be able explain what you are doing with third-party data, how you reach the results and any steps you take to mitigate any potential bias.

Getting started

The first step is to develop your conceptual use cases for AI. These need only be at high level to start. When you have three to five ideas, consider the data you have available or can acquire, and the type of insights you want to glean. Alternatively, you may be considering using commercially available tools to augment human activities. If that is the case, get a demonstration of the tool, satisfy yourself that it would be helpful and understand if there are any critical dependencies to using the tool.

This analysis aligning the data to the vision and/or assessing tools will give you an idea of which concepts are viable. You can then flesh out a high-level operating model which contemplates how you will use AI to augment the unique human capabilities of emotional intelligence, critical and abstract thinking and comprehension of the context and nuance of the spoken word.

You need to think ahead. I suggest 6-12 months if you want to use AI for improved customer engagement, 9-18 months if the use pertains to greater personalisation of services and probably 2 years or more if you are seeking to gain unique insights from data. If you already have thousands of lines of well-organised data then you can subtract 6-12 months from the timelines for the personalisation and unique insight applications. I have reviewed hundreds of AI projects. Probably over three quarters of them fail before they start as there is no plan for the data acquisition and management. If there is one final message it is to treasure any data you have, store it securely, organise it consistently – treat it like gold dust, it is the new fuel of business.

CHAPTER 4:

Does AI Know You Better Than You Know Yourself?

Intuition

I worked as a business consultant for over twenty years, leading my own company. As a company we were extremely fortunate that all our work came from my direct network or by referral. Consequently, we spent most of our time on client assignments rather than marketing or pitching.

This meant I personally was gaining huge experience and learning nearly every day. When I reflect on this time and how people reacted to me and what they said about me, it's quite interesting. In the early years, the comments were typically focussed on operational delivery and how we got on with the extended team at the clients. In the latter years one comment really struck me: "John can write the minutes of the meeting in advance of the meeting."

I am not unique in being able to read a situation and anticipate the outcome; it comes to all of us with experience. It is this lifetime of learning that trains us and develops our intuition. We each receive thousands or maybe millions of pieces of information every day. We learn from all of these each time we pass someone in the street, cross a road, every conversation etc. I discussed some of these signals and how they facilitate social interaction in Chapter 2. This is what gives us a rounded judgment capability and differentiates us from AI, which is typically good at the one very narrow task that it is trained to do.

AI is trained to address a specific task, maybe identifying a feeling, predicting a behaviour or recognising an object. It is possible to have multiple AIs working together; for example, driverless cars are controlled by a collection of AIs each performing specific tasks. However, it still is a long way short of human capability.

Microsoft's Tay bot is often cited as a demonstration of the limitations of AI's learning capability. Tay was launched on Twitter as an AI teenager. The idea was that Tay would learn how to interact when it observed other conversations on Twitter. Tay could only process text and not understand it, it typically reworded things it had seen to keep the conversation going. Consequently, Tay became offensive and racist, tweeting many inappropriate remarks, so it had to be withdrawn after 24 hours.

AI doesn't have intuition based on the full range of learnings humans have with other people and their environment. Intuition is a fundamental aspect that sets humans and probably most intelligent animals apart from machines and computers. You have intuition; therefore you will be able to harness AI and this is why I believe that AI offers you great opportunities. But, be aware: AI is as good or better than any psychologist, psychiatrist or psychoanalyst at understanding specific aspects of how you feel or what you do.

Predicting the future

We all want to know aspects of the future. For example, what the weather will be like at the weekend, whether the stock market will rise or fall, what will be the hot fashion item next year, etc. I find it hard to believe that AI is going to be able to help us significantly with any of these challenges in the short to medium term. I don't believe that we, as the human race, understand how to define all the problems AI will need to solve to make these predictions reliable. I also doubt if there is adequate, consistent data.

Even though AI may not be a good predictor of the future I do think it is good at predicting some aspects of human behaviour. If you have ever made a purchase based on a recommendation from Amazon or Netflix, then AI has predicted your future purchasing behaviour. AI is very good at understanding people and postulating what they may do or who they may like. The reason it is so good at this is because there are substantial data sets to learn from and people can be categorised. This categorisation enables the AI to present a view of future behaviour. AI is so much better than me or you at this as it has the power to process so much more data quicker. If you work in marketing, you may well have been segmenting the market without too much granularity and defining potential product-market matches for specific segments. AI makes this process more granular, more dynamic and more accurate. The consequence of this is that AI probably does know more about what we may end up buying than we do ourselves. Remember my example with the chandeliers from Chapter 1.

Sentiment analysis

The use of AI to classify a piece of text is well established. There are numerous commercially available products that use it to assess Tweets and other social media posts. These are widely used, especially by the big brands. Over the last two to three years I found that if I was receiving bad service it was sometimes better to mention it on Twitter than to the poor person on the customer service desk. Twitter is continuously monitored by the brands, and Tweets that have negative sentiment are flagged and attended to, quickly.

I remember my brother-in-law telling me about a long wait he had in a car dealership for his car to be returned after being serviced. He became frustrated after thirty minutes and asked the customer service person to fetch the manager. No manager appeared, so he tweeted about being kept waiting at the specific car dealership. Within five minutes the dealer principal came over to him to understand and resolve the problem!

The above case is an example where the level of negative sentiment in my brother-in-law's Tweet exceeded a threshold set in the AI, hence it was flagged for immediate attention. Many more Tweets will be less extreme. By using AI to assess them all for sentiment it is possible for brand managers to get a good view on the feelings towards their brand at a point in time.

Polls and questionnaires have been used for many years to determine voting habits or to receive structured data on the aspects of a service people liked or disliked. You may be familiar with the promoter score, which asks how likely you are to recommend a product or service to a friend. Many companies judge the person delivering the service on this score. Have you ever been asked to give a 9 or a 10 by the person delivering the score? That is why! However, is this really a good thing? The person you or I engage with may well be doing their best but other aspects of the company's service may be poor. Consequently, you may provide feedback to support the person you dealt with rather than on your overall experience.

AI can be used to address this and similar challenges. It can glean sentiment from unstructured data, ie free text.

This means that (for example) surveys could be changed to ask a few open questions, such as "Please tell me what you liked about our service" or "Please tell me what you didn't like."

I think the concept of asking people to say what they think rather than just ticking boxes can enable greater understanding of product/service-to-market fit and customer sentiment. One of the beauties of AI is that it works by statistical comparison so it could read a piece of text and then return positive and negative scores rather than just 'good' or 'bad'.

Team dynamics

There will be ethical questions in how far this can be taken. For example, you may send emails to colleagues and communicate with them on an instant messenger service like MS Teams, Webex or Slack. How much of a step is it for these to be analysed for sentiment towards the company or the team? If this were legal and possible, then how good would the analysis really be? Would it deliver a better understanding of the team dynamics than an astute manager with well-developed emotional intelligence?

This line of argument takes me to an important point: how good is AI really at determining sentiment? For short pieces of written text, it is helpful. Twitter is a great example as there is a character limit of 280 characters (roughly 50 words); survey responses will also likely be short. However, for longer pieces of prose that cover many themes it is probably of limited help as there will be many themes and points covered, some of which may be contradictory.

Turning back to the team dynamics, team members probably interact face-to-face too. As they will be able to see each other's faces and body language they can gauge their interactions according to how they feel. Maybe some of these will be passive-aggressive, maybe some will be incredibly collaborative – AI is unlikely to determine this.

How do you feel?

Behaviomedics is the science of using subtle human signals to determine wellbeing. Apps are being developed to use face and voice recognition techniques to detect subtle changes in facial muscle action and voice tone to determine mental wellbeing. This science will enable patients to better manage their own mental-health wellbeing. The subtleties identified by behaviomedics provide objective measures. The patient can take a measurement when it suits them thus eliminating the stressful situation associated with an assessment in the clinician's office.

PainChek is an Australian company that is using face recognition to score pain. At the moment the clinician asks the patient to score pain on a subjective scale of 1–10. They repeat this question throughout the treatment or surgery recovery programme and see if it reduces. This means that readings are taken at a snapshot in time. Using apps like PainChek, patients could be asked to take three measurements per day (for example) and the trend over time can be measured.

BlueSkeye is a UK-based company that uses face recognition techniques to score depression. Their product, TrueBlue, has been calibrated against the questionnaires that are currently used to assess depression. This enables patients to take readings at regular intervals and provide the clinician with better information on their overall wellbeing.

It isn't just our faces that give tell-tale signs of how we feel. Our voices do too. The German company Audeering analyses sounds, including voices, to determine how people feel. It uses AI to determine the environment someone is in, how they are interacting with others and over 50 emotional states. The technology can be readily integrated into many platforms, mobile phones, wearables, computers, etc so potentially can give users live feedback on others' feelings as they go about their daily business.

The larger technology companies are researching deeper into the topic. IBM is using its Watson AI technology to analyse clinicians' notes and transcripts from patient interviews. IBM's vision is that by the middle of this decade, patterns in our speech and written word will provide early indicators of behavioural disorders, psychosis, schizophrenia and degenerative brain disease.

Helping us cope

As well as recognition and diagnosis of anxiety, AI also has a role in the development of management plans, especially those based on Cognitive Behavioural Therapy (CBT) and

Mindfulness. AI is a component in numerous apps that provide meditation support and aid sleep.

Headspace acquired a voice recognition company so that is could glean more detailed insights into how its customers were feeling and then provide more bespoke advice. Calm uses AI to recognise patterns in users' answers and is also innovating on using it to write stories, based on fairy tales, that will help users relax. There are other well-known apps in this space: Wysa, Youper and Woebot. Woebot provides a 'companion' that uses AI to provide coaching so users can use CBT techniques to reduce their levels of anxiety. Wysa and Youper take the approach of being a personal therapist and asking the user questions to help them understand their feelings. The direction of the conversation is derived using AI.

Being nosey

I believe that the use of AI to understand people's feelings warrants public debate about ethical usage. I think that the narrow scope of each AI application means that your deepest private thoughts and feelings are unlikely to be compromised. However, as time goes on, you and many others may want greater assurance that your privacy isn't being eroded.

What I will do is map out possible usage models that could develop over the next few years, based on these uses of AI and other technologies that are readily available. These scenarios may trouble you a little more.

A few years ago Google demonstrated glasses (spectacles) that would provide users with more information about their surroundings. These weren't a success, but the concept is still finding its way. Snapchat sells glasses that offer an enhanced and more immersive experience. Apple is rumoured to be about to offer glasses that will probably be more for the augmented reality market, which is discussed later in this book.

Notwithstanding that, if these devices facilitate the use of apps that detect mood you could obtain real-time feedback on how you are making someone feel. Similarly, you could use voice recognition technology to monitor phone calls or instructions to Alexa, Google Home or other voice-activated assistants. On the face of it, you may feel that this will help you be more empathetic. However, could others exploit this information for less worthy purposes?

These applications of AI are already being used on companion robots to determine levels of engagement or frustration. This will only be the tip of the iceberg. As these robots become common in all walks of life, they will have input on our mood and temperament. That in itself is probably not a threat, but who has access to the data collected by the robot? What could they use it for?

Joining the dots

Extrapolate this a step further: the FAANGs are moving into other markets, such as banking with Apple and Android pay; could they go further and move into mental health monitoring? Just think about how much data they could collect if they integrated these technologies with their own. All of this data would be stored in their global clouds. The speeds of 5G will mean that people will be depositing data into the cloud as though they are interacting locally with other people or their own mobile device.

The FAANGs already collect a huge amount of data about us. As discussed previously, they use it to predict what we might buy, who we may like or things we may want to do. What happens if they add to this mental health data? Does that enable them to sell treatments and therapies? Would that be ethical if someone with a mental health issue was vulnerable?

How do you really feel about there being a minute-by-minute monitoring of your mental wellbeing and your social skills? How can this be controlled and really only used beneficially? These are questions that our society will need to answer over the coming months and years. Given the scale of the mental health challenge worldwide, I believe that AI is the only viable scalable solution but it needs to come with significant understanding and guidance on ethical operating models.

I have no doubt that understanding feelings will provide society with significant benefit. My concern is that people should be sufficiently aware to understand how their information is used and to 'turn off' some of the capture and analysis functions if they so choose.

I must return to the point of this chapter: is AI better than humans at understanding other people? I still believe that the answer is an emphatic 'NO'. AI can provide great insight into a few aspects of how we think and feel, and can provide better objective data for clinicians and psychology experts to make their diagnosis. However, it doesn't have, and probably won't have any time soon, the gut-feel or intuition that you have.

CHAPTER 5:

Truth, Lies, Scams and Fakes

Gullible us

Since the beginning of time, trying to decide if someone is telling the truth or if something is real has been a cornerstone of our societal existence. People have pretended to be others and misled others. The propaganda machines of both the free and oppressed worlds have continually painted a picture of how much better life is under their governance, and people have been taken in by financial scams that have proliferated on both a large scale and individual level.

My observation is that if a news article, advert or conversation enforces someone's beliefs, appears to solve a problem for them, or appeals to the emotions of greed or fear, then people are likely to believe it.

Nothing new

It seems that even the collective intelligence of the masses is no protection from these schemes. In the 1700s many, many people lost money investing in the stock market, based on the promises of the South Sea Company. The South Sea Bubble, as it is known, was a classic case of herd greed and it cost the UK dear. The artificially inflated values of company stocks enticed many people to buy stock in not only the South Sea Company, but also in other fanciful ventures. When it became apparent that the South Sea Company and many others of these ventures weren't delivering financial returns through their trading, the stock market collapsed.

You may recall the dot com bubble and crash between about 1995 and 2002. The excitement associated with internet companies in the late 1990s caused their valuations to be based on new metrics rather than profitability and cash flow. This caused their stock price to rise significantly. However, in 2001 the investment community became concerned that expectations weren't realistic and consequently share prices crashed. The US technology-laden Nasdaq index collapsed by nearly 80%.

Unlike the South Sea Bubble, there wasn't the feeling that there had been mass deception. However, there was an energy company, Enron, that suffered a significant fall from grace at that time. This was determined to have been due to deceit and in fact led to the collapse of not just Enron, but also their auditors, Arthur Andersen.

You may well have been exposed to pyramid selling schemes, where people pay a fee to join the scheme and may receive a product or service (typically of low value) in return. Participants receive a payment for each new person they persuade to join the scheme. Therefore, as money comes into the scheme it is used to pay recruiters and some flow up the pyramid to the founders and more senior members.

Pyramid selling is illegal in many countries even though it is different from a Ponzi scheme, which offers investors an attractive return. What the investors may not realise is that this return is funded by new investment coming into the scheme, rather than the performance of the underlying assets. Consequently, when the level of new investment falls below the levels required to pay existing investors the scheme collapses.

You may conclude that the current situation with deep fakes, fake news, banking scams and increasing levels of fraud are nothing new. You would be right, but what AI does is enable both (i) these dishonest practices to proliferate and (ii) the development of tools to check the veracity of these claims. Some people talk about the speed of development of these two opposed AI capabilities as similar to the arms race between the East and the West after World War II.

Do I trust him or her?

We make up our minds about whether someone is telling the truth or not through gut feel. We may believe that we use a range of techniques to underpin our intuition. Some of the data points we may consider include: is what they are saying plausible? Do they look confident? Do they look us in the eyes? Are they speaking too quickly or two slowly? Are they shuffling about? Etc.

Lie detector tests have been around for a while. They measure physiological signals to determine if someone is anxious. If they are, it assumes they are lying. There is only limited use of this equipment, as the results are deemed dubious. From what I can see lie detectors haven't been accepted in law or by society as a whole. I don't believe that AI will change this anytime soon. I feel that AI will help in specific use cases, by providing an assessment of the veracity of claims and provenance of information. I do not see this leading to a general lie detection test, though.

An area where AI is particularly useful is monitoring phone calls in the financial services sector. After the 2008 financial crisis, regulations on banks and other companies trading financial assets were tightened considerably. All phone calls had to be recorded. Teams of compliance staff used to listen to randomly selected calls to determine if they were dishonest or not. The AI tools enable a more selective choice of calls for further investigation. The technology assesses each call and provides a statistical probability of its being fraudulent. The compliance team then only listen to those above a certain threshold.

AI can be trained to recognise aspects of a conversation that could indicate a level of deceit. These may include how quickly someone is talking, whether they use certain phrases, repetition and use of language.

Deceit or the truth

The thrust of the argument is that if someone isn't telling the truth, then AI may detect signs of anxiety associated with being deceitful. There are many situations where people say something that is incorrect but they genuinely believe it to be true at the time.

The press takes great pride in trying to demonstrate that certain politicians in the free world ubiquitously don't speak the truth. The reality is that many politicians talk at high level and the details on the ground don't quite match. This probably doesn't count as being untruthful as the politician may genuinely believe that if his or her advisors say something will be delivered, then they have the plans in place to do so.

Politicians are in the public eye and often recorded. I think it should be possible, in the foreseeable future to use AI to assess consistency of behaviour, mannerisms and style of speaking. The AI could detect changes in mannerisms and speech patterns and flag up specific differences. Over time these could be attributed to points that clearly were untrue and may be an indicator of less than honest intent.

It may not be him or her

Staying with the political theme I do believe we will see AI playing a malevolent role. A few years ago Jordan Peele and Buzzfeed produced a video of Barack Obama delivering a public service address about fake news. It is alarming how realistic the video and voiceover are.

A UK think tank, Future Advocacy, put out videos during the 2019 UK general election campaign. The two contenders for Prime Minister, Boris Johnson and Jeremy Corbyn appeared to endorse each other. While the videos and voiceovers weren't perfect, it made the point that good quality fakes can be produced quickly.

The proliferation of video footage means that the producers of deep fakes have plenty of raw material to build on. The worry is that the deep fakes can be used to influence elections, especially as there are simpler alternatives to producing a full-blown speech. For example: making someone appear to slur their speech or fail to articulate something clearly. In 2019 a video circulated of House Speaker, Nancy Pelosi, where she appeared to be drunk or ill discussing President Trump's refusal to cooperate with Congress's investigation. In fact, the video had been slowed down, and millions of Americans viewed it. UK politicians have also had their deep fake challenges. In the 2019 election Keir Starmer seemed to appear uncertain of his position on Brexit in an interview. Again, this was later proven to be a doctored video.

Fake videos have been produced for years. Often, these contain grainy or blurred images. With the advent of high-quality fakes, it is becoming necessary to use technology to detect them. This has become a race, similar to that between the producers of computer viruses and those who produce anti-virus software. This new 'arms race' is serious business. Facebook, Microsoft and leading universities in the US and UK are co-ordinating a challenge to develop technology that will detect if videos have been doctored.

Prevention is better than cure

Researchers are investigating prevention too. The Albany, State University of New York leads the field in adding noise patterns to videos. This additional noise isn't discernible by the human eye. It alters the pixel patterns in the frame and reduces the effectiveness of the software producing the fake video by obscuring facial images and adding decoys. This means that the face recognition software producing the deep fake has fewer real faces and more duds to learn from, meaning it is less effective. Professor Siwei Lyu leads this work. He hopes that, one day, whenever you upload a video to social media, you will be given the opportunity to protect it.

Until this time arrives, there are a few things you can do to mitigate the risk of being duped by deep fakes. The first is to consider if it really makes sense: how likely is it that a senior politician campaigning for election is drunk? It is also worth looking at the background in the video to see if that is appropriate to the circumstances. Does the whole scenario seem plausible? The next is to look at the quality: does the mouth really move in sync with the spoken word?

Is the voice really that of the person in the video? Maybe check some alternative voice clips to see if the tone and accent match. The third is to look for correlating evidence: if there is an immediate denial from the person in the video then that should lead to doubt that the video is real.

Should I believe it?

Fake news seems to spread through social media faster than real news. I think the general public became more aware of fake news during the 2016 US Presidential election. The successful candidate, who wasn't a politician, constantly referred to fake news to deflect the criticism he received in the press. Whether you like or dislike Donald Trump, he does have a point.

Just look at your Facebook or Twitter feed, or even the news articles selected by Google in its feed if you have an Android phone; some seem to contradict each other and others seem to be beyond belief.

One of the benefits of having a free press is that journalists can publish what they think fit as long as they can point to a genuine source and prove that they have taken reasonable steps to validate the story. Even with these professional standards there are often stories that appear to conflict with each other in the main news channels. Sometimes this is due to different interpretations by the journalists, other times it is due to conflicting sources of information.

Social media greatly facilitate the spread of news and opinions. They have far greater reach and appeal than the traditional media and are also more immediate. New actors are springing up all the time and constructing news stories that can be placed into feeds, or even shared through fake accounts. These actors may even mimic credible sites to make their articles appear more authentic. Sometimes these placements on social media are supported by automated accounts, bots, which may even enter into the dialogue on the article with comments posted underneath.

Facebook and Twitter actively use AI techniques to identify fake accounts, bots and other data patterns that could indicate fraudulent activity or the spread of fake news. These techniques include machine learning looking for contextual anomalies and Natural Language Processing (NLP) to identify the 'linguistic fingerprint' of articles, which may give an indication of whether they are from a known source, legitimate or malevolent, that writes with a particular style.

I think that this battle with fake news will probably never be won: trends in human behaviour render us more susceptible to believing fake news. Do you prefer to consume soundbites rather than read long articles? Do you also find you frequently are doing something else when you scan news articles? This means that you may be more likely to click on a link in the article if it seems interesting. It could be click-bait and lead you to a more extreme article, or worse.

As society becomes more polarised, fault lines become more evident and views held become more extreme. The 2016 US election and UK referendum on Brexit are indicators of how the different sectors of society are becoming more entrenched and less motivated to participate in reasoned debate. You may find it more comfortable to read material that reinforces your beliefs, as opposed to taking time to understand and challenge alternative perspectives.

We see a greater lack of trust in, and support for, 'the Establishment'. I personally think that it is right that the authorities and the major companies that derive so much benefit from our society are held to account. To my mind, social media have made a great contribution in developing this accountability. However, when articles are false and pernicious this is unhelpful as we all need these organisations to be able to function effectively. In order for the public to be able to be persuasive and hold these organisations to account, they need to be well informed with facts and reasoned opinion. Therefore, it is in all our interests that society in general becomes more sensitive to fake news.

Earlier in the book I made the case that, if you are to succeed and feel fulfilled as AI proliferates in society, you will need to apply your emotional intelligence and critical thinking to information you receive. Falling into the trap of believing fake news would run counter to this.

I hope you find the following tips useful when assessing the veracity of news articles you see. Look at the general appearance of the article: is it from a source you are familiar with? Is the presentation consistent with the source? Look beyond the headline and consider how the article is written, is the style similar to other articles from that author? Does the article present its case in a balanced or extreme manner? Does the quality of grammar reflect a professional standard? Are there spelling mistakes?

A harder thing to do is to consider your own biases and beliefs: do you favour or dislike the article because you align to its views? This is a really hard test, as you may have strong conviction that your views are right. There is nothing wrong with that. However, just because an article doesn't align to your views doesn't mean it is fake news; you just consider the arguments incorrect. If you want to see how different the views in society are on the topics of the day, try buying half a dozen different daily papers and see how their interpretation of the news of the day differs. If you wish to understand whether you have biases you may be unaware about, see which articles you find easiest to read.

You can also look externally to validate news articles. A Google check of the author should provide information on them and other articles they have penned; a Google search for other articles on the same topic could provide suitable validation. Finally, there are fact checker sites such as snopes.com and factchecker.org that are regarded as credible sources for validation.

Catching me out

You may have noticed that one of the recurring themes is that AI 'industrialises' processes that we already have. It enables a repetitive activity done by humans, for example, reading a piece of text to assign a sentiment, to be undertaken many hundreds or thousands of times over in a short time period.

While there are many 'good' uses, it also helps scammers extend their reach and sophistication. You may already be wary of emails with requests to log in on a link that purports to come from your bank. Often these emails present your bank's logo and branding. AI will enable the quality of these fakes to continually improve, the messages will become more compelling and may even be specific to you, and if you are in a hurry you may be inclined to click the link.

Scammers are clever, they know that if they inject a sense of urgency and panic then the user is more likely to click on a link. Recently, I received a text from my credit card company advising that they had spotted some suspicious activity on my account. They provided a link in the text that supposedly enabled me to talk to a customer service agent. Fortunately, I have apps on my phone for my credit card and bank accounts so I thought I would look quickly to see what they were talking about. I couldn't see any unauthorised transactions, so instead of clicking the link I rang the usual customer services number. You guessed it, it was a scam.

While financial services companies will develop systems to try and counter these scams I think that it will ultimately be up to you and me to change our behaviours. We will need to become more distrusting of any requests for payment or action until we have verified them. This means we will have to subordinate convenience to assurance. This cynicism may also need to be applied to news articles and video clips. If I relate this to the purpose of the book, to help you do well in the next decade as AI proliferates, I must encourage you to develop critical thinking techniques and not embrace a mindset of cynicism.

Undoubtedly this chapter has highlighted an unintended consequence of AI: it will slow down some of our actions as we need to validate the information we receive. Having said that, I have outlined in earlier chapters how AI will help us live our lives. I am now going to discuss how AI can help you in your work, your hobbies, and your life generally. I am hopeful you will conclude that the benefits outweigh the challenges.

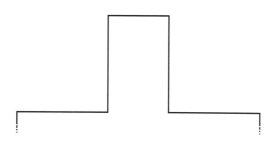

PART 3

HOW YOU CAN USE AI

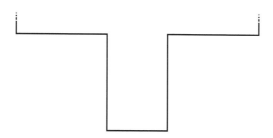

CHAPTER 6:

Will a Computer Steal My Job?

Job insecurity is the norm

Over the last 30 years we have become used to seeing more and more traditional jobs disappear. It hasn't all been doom and gloom as other jobs have appeared, sometimes as the result of this automation. Notwithstanding the 2020 coronavirus pandemic, jobs seem to always be available in hospitality, leisure, tourism, wellbeing, the care sector and distribution. However, these roles typically have little or no job security or employment benefits associated with them and are poorly paid.

The changes to employment in society are caused by a number of factors, changing customer preferences, globalisation and automation.

Going shopping

Amazon started in 1994, selling books online. Later that decade it broadened the portfolio and started to become a major force in online retailing. Not only did other firms start as online retailers and marketplaces, but traditional High Street retailers found they had to follow suit and establish an online presence. This meant that by the turn of the century customers could purchase everything from their weekly grocery shop to IT online. The shift to online shopping has been gradual. Many people still prefer to select their food, especially fresh produce, in store. They may also wish to try on clothes and check out the performance of some electrical goods, eg televisions, before they buy them. However, generous returns policies, improving quality standards, busy lifestyles and an increase in the spending power of millennials and generation Z (as they enter into work and develop their careers) has seen the percentage of online sales gradually increase over time.

Globalisation and outsourcing

You have almost certainly spoken with a call centre in India, especially if you call your bank or a utility company. Did you realise that when you speak to a service desk engineer, maybe for your phone company or an IT company, you may be speaking with someone in Mexico or Egypt?

There has also been a trend for more skilled jobs, especially in the IT and procurement sectors, to be placed overseas. Cisco, for example, has its largest R&D hub, outside of California, in Bangalore. Software is often developed and/or coded in eastern European countries. Many now have a thriving, albeit small (when compared to G7 countries) IT sector. These hubs tend to evolve around universities. Krakow in Poland is an important hub, Prague (Czech Republic), Tallinn (Estonia) and Budapest (Hungary) also boast capabilities; Lviv in Ukraine is emerging rapidly into the mainstream.

Back office roles that are mostly process-oriented have been offshored too; for example, many household name banks have procurement centres in West Asia and South America.

This trend to offshoring has incurred some political and social backlash but this has not abated the flow of work overseas. The cost dynamics of labour arbitrage have been compelling for organisations that operate on a global scale. Having said that, the gap is closing slowly, so over the last few years there has been an increase in the combination of nearshoring and offshoring models.

The professions aren't immune either: law firms in the UK no longer need to be owned by lawyers. Businesspeople can establish a registered law firm, as long as there is a clear process to ensure accountability for the advice given, and professional indemnity insurance in case things go wrong. Entrepreneurs in countries familiar with the English common law system found they could undertake low-level legal work (commercial contracts, basic litigation, etc) for major companies. If you work for, or deal with, a global bank or telecoms company you may find you are dealing with a lawyer in India or South Africa.

Automation

Earlier in the book I discussed the automation of car plants. Other factories and warehouses have also been automated by robotic machines. Automation is touching much more of our daily lives now. If you check in at an airport you may find that you are asked to check in at a terminal yourself and weigh, tag and deposit your luggage yourself, using a machine. You may contact a company and talk to an automated chatbot. Almost inevitably, when you telephone a call centre you will speak with an auto-attendant. Computers replace bookkeeping clerks. The way automation is eroding jobs is apparent to us all.

What will be the impact of AI? Will it accelerate automation to the point where there are very few jobs? Will it exacerbate or alter the labour arbitrage trend? What jobs will go? Where may jobs be created? How do you reduce your risk of being another unemployment or redundancy statistic? I will answer these questions in this part of the book.

Anxiety

Over the last twenty years I have developed a perception that the people I work with on projects in large companies are increasingly unhappy, insecure in their jobs and less motivated. I get the impression that many of them feel they have to justify their department's or their own existence. I also discern that consequently there are increased levels of anxiety. This insight came from my narrow, albeit global view of the world.

In 2018, David Graeber, the leading anthropologist, published a highly acclaimed book, *Bullshit Jobs*. He contends that over half of jobs are pointless and that this is having a detrimental psychological effect on society, especially when paired with a work ethic that associates work with self-worth. If I extrapolate David's conclusion into the world of AI, I see initially a massive resistance to change and using AI, especially at scale. Employees, even if they are doing jobs they feel are pointless, need to work and make a living. They will feel they are literally fighting for their lives.

I have seen this toxic culture develop in the workplace first-hand. I, thankfully, have been able to stand back from it, as my engagement was as an external adviser. One of my motivations for writing this book is to help you rise above this frustration. I think that AI will create new opportunities, many that are fulfilling, especially for folks who embrace the technology.

History does support this argument: in the past, when there has been a quantum leap in industrialisation or automation, economies have become more productive and net jobs have increased.

Industrial revolutions create jobs

AI is regarded by many as the 'fourth industrial revolution'. I concur that it will change the nature of work beyond recognition.

Two of the previous three industrial revolutions predated my life. The first was in the mid-eighteenth century, with the advent of mechanisation and the invention of the steam engine. Initially the use of static steam engines enabled more mining efficiency. Many mills, used for manufacturing, were sited by rivers and used the water flow to power them. Steam engines offered the option to place factories in more locations.

Steam engine companies proliferated, accelerating the development of steam engines so they could be used in a wider variety of settings. These included transport, where they were the enabling technology for the transformation of railways, boats and agricultural equipment.

The evolution of the transport sector facilitated the creation of more markets and jobs. For example, passenger trips on steamboats, both for leisure and business. Quicker transport by railway (railroad) meant that supply chains didn't need to be in such close proximity to the manufacturer or their markets. This enabled existing industries to expand and serve new markets.

Moving forward 100 years, there was the development of the internal combustion engine and the use of fossil fuels. This transformed the emerging electricity sector and personal transport. A quote often attributed to Henry Ford, the founder of Ford motor cars, is "If I had asked people what they wanted they would have said faster horses". This exemplifies the need for new thinking and innovation so we can make maximum use of new technology.

The internal combustion engine has been truly revolutionary; this technology is used to propel cars, buses, military equipment, aeroplanes, boats, etc. Jobs were created to manufacture, service and market the vehicles and equipment. Additionally, being able to transport people and goods cost effectively has been the foundation of much of the global economy for more than the last century. You may wish to reflect on all the market sectors that depend on, and have been enabled by, transport. Overseas holidays is an example that may be top of mind.

Each industrial revolution is the foundation for the next

The third industrial revolution, computers/IT occurred another hundred years on, in the 1970s. Computers became mainstream but weren't easy to use. I remember starting a PC, putting the floppy drive in and going through the text-based dialogue to reach my word processing program. There was no Windows operating system, it was something called DOS. There was no Microsoft Office or G Suite. We had WordStar, and then WordPerfect. There were no internet or multi-media communication tools.

In the 1980s Apple came to the fore, providing a PC with a more user-friendly operating system. I remember being thrilled when I joined a new company in 1988 and they gave me my own Apple Macintosh to use! The 1980s also saw the birth of the mobile phone. My first phone (which was provided by my employer) had its own carry handle and was really best used in the car. No text messages or data downloads in those days, though! The 1990s saw the birth of the internet and the rise of the Windows PC. PCs and mobile phones proliferated; however, compared to today's devices, they were still primitive.

In parallel with these developments we saw the exponential expansion of a massive new industry – IT. Software developers, PC and cable installers (no wifi then), IT services staff, etc were required by every organisation. Major organisations created IT departments, many with board-level accountability. With the development of the internet in the early 2000s we saw a whole range of spin-off industries providing services over the internet. Initially these were information services and public email providers. Then, everyone had to have a website, so website development became a new work opportunity. This led to growth of online retail, as everybody could have a website, and so the job creation goes on.

As we moved through the 2000s, mobile telecoms technology has been greatly enhanced. You will be used to watching video on your mobile devices. Twenty years ago, this wasn't possible. With the advent of 5G technology you will soon be able to enjoy an improved gaming experience on your device. This means that we can often work and socialise remotely and in fact select where we choose to be to do these things.

As mobile network technology has been developed, use cases for this capability have boomed. There are now over 2 million apps available, providing access to powerful IT-based services from your smartphone. This is another example how an industrial revolution creates jobs. Each of these apps were created by somebody or a company; the services they provide access to were developed and are delivered by people in gainful employment.

You may have devices in your home – security cameras, light switches, child monitors, heating controls, etc – that are connected to the internet. This has evolved into something called 'the Internet of Things' (IoT). This in turn means that there are vast amounts of data to store and manage, so we have the data centre sector, which needs ultra-high security, meaning more technology and more jobs. As we enter the 2020s we are at a point where we have so much data we don't know what to do with it!

Since the advent of GPUs (graphics processing units) for gaming, computers and servers can now, cost effectively, be provided with sufficient power to undertake the computations necessary to develop AI programs.

AI: the fourth industrial revolution

I believe that the 2020s will be the decade in which AI really makes its mark. I don't think for one minute that you will see the development of general AI that leads to robots taking over the world. What I believe you will see is the advent of intelligent tools which will be used to fulfil many routine aspects of our daily life. These tools will also help you make better decisions quicker and glean insight that wasn't previously possible.

AI is much, much more than IT: it offers some cognitive functions too – it is capable of reasoning; it also has sensory perception – it can detect mood and honesty, it can engage in conversation, it can recognise faces, it can even smell. It works differently from the IT we are used to, which is hard programmed to go through a fixed routine. It learns from data and consequently can improve its output over time.

The reality

However, like many new technologies it is overhyped at the moment. Gartner, the research company, publishes what it calls 'the hype cycle' for new technologies. It argues that as a technology is researched and developed it goes through five stages before becoming widely adopted:

1. Innovation – when there are new ideas and research is well underway.

2. Peak of inflated expectation – when the press find out about the new technology and everyone gets overly excited about what they think it will do.

3. Trough of disillusionment – when people realise what it can't do.

4. Slope of enlightenment – when the technology matures to become operationally viable and people's expectations become realistic.

5. Plateau – when people can use the technology to do useful things.

There are probably 50 or more sub-categories of AI. For argument's sake, let's take 2015 as a general starting point. AI developments are taking 2–5 years to reach the peak of inflated expectation and the trough of disillusionment; very few have reached the slope of enlightenment yet.

This ties in with what I see in the market: (i) a few well-developed applications such as: predicting buying behaviour, identifying customer sentiment and preferences, face and speech recognition for security purposes and predictive maintenance programs, and (ii) point programs for specific applications, such as: menu-based dialogue at call centres, basic repetitive robotic functions (for example in a warehouse) and to help focus an operator's workload (for example filtering out compliance cases that don't need checking).

One area, though, that is really taking off is Robotic Process Automation (RPA). As AI is intelligent, it can filter and merge data much more effectively than the current script-driven processes – these fail if there isn't absolute data uniformity. RPA can be thought of as a software robot that mimics human activity. I often liken it to a data entry clerk, typing at a keyboard. These people are not completely script-driven, as they notice if something looks odd, but not every time. This type of work is soul destroying as it requires considerable attention to detail but is boring. The sort of applications they undertake includes reporting and writing to databases, merging, and transferring records, invoice processing, insurance claims processing and IT services support.

This could be scary

As with the other industrial revolutions, there will be winners and losers. You may have heard the saying (wrongly) attributed to Charles Darwin, the English scientist who espoused the theory of evolution: "It isn't the strongest of the species that survives, nor the most intelligent that survives. It is the one that is most adaptable to change." I believe that this is so true with AI: clearly AI will remove much routine from our lives, therefore routine jobs will be at risk. However, AI will cause new jobs to be created. I think that as a society we are only just beginning to understand how it could enable new business models, and the AI industry itself is still in its infancy.

I encourage you to think of the impact AI will have on your job prospects in three planes. There are physical and white-collar jobs that are the same, day in, day out. These are certainly vulnerable, some of them almost immediately. There are other jobs that have a routine component but also a higher-value component – this is probably the vast range of white-collar employment. Then, there are jobs which have little routine, involve well-developed critical thinking and emotional intelligence, and probably a fair bit of creativity too. I will look at each of these groups in turn and discuss the respective risks associated with each of them.

Time to start looking for something else

Repetitive physical work can readily be taken over by robots – manufacturing has been exploiting robot technology for many years. The factory line is a completely 'set' environment, so assembly robots can be set up to work in exactly the same place every time; they don't need to think or adjust. AI empowers robots further: they can be equipped with recognition technologies so they know where to find items and can 'see' where to place them. However, safety is a major concern, especially if they operate alongside a human workforce.

Extrapolating from the factory floor to the warehouse, we can get a better idea of how robots, robotic devices and people can work together. Amazon has been using robotic arms for a while to stack pallets and lift heavy loads; they now use mobile robots to select items and bring them to packers. Some jobs have been replaced, but new jobs have been created to run and support the robots. The increased throughput at these fulfilment centres is creating employment opportunities, both at Amazon and in its supply chain.

Moving to the white-collar roles that are most at risk. I mentioned Robotic Process Automation earlier. These are software robots (bots) that manipulate data, typically passing it between systems and data stores. Developing these bots for specific tasks is quite straight forward when there is sufficient historic data available that has previously been sorted or organised. If you are responsible for data collection, data entry or repetitive data processing, I'm afraid the situation isn't a case of 'if' you will be replaced, but 'when'.

I mentioned globalisation and outsourcing earlier and how much of this is undertaken overseas. Therefore, I will consider the challenge of potential mass redundancy at a global level rather than just in my London, UK bubble. In the UK, much repetitive physical work is undertaken by immigrants from Commonwealth countries and Eastern Europe. Much of the data processing work is outsourced overseas. Who does this work and where it gets done is to some degree irrelevant. These roles contribute to the fabric and running of our society, so I believe we should consider if and how they could be repurposed. The good news is that I believe AI will create new opportunities, both as an industry in its own right, and by enabling other industries. Some of these new roles could be ideal for components of our extended society that are replaced by AI. Please hold this thought, I will return to it later in the book.

Time to think about your future job

Most white-collar jobs will change, some will be augmented by AI and the only difference will be a greater degree of accountability. Others will change more fundamentally and may not bear much similarity to what you do today apart, perhaps, from the overall purpose of the role or department you work in.

A good exemplar to start with is IT services. When you get a problem with your work computer or phone you probably log a case with the help desk using an online system. You describe the fault and assign a level of priority. The level of priority determines how long it takes to get a response and the nature of that response. If the matter is complex and/or high priority you may well get a phone call or an agent to contact you on the company's instant messaging service. If the matter is lower priority you may receive an email response with a list of actions.

Some companies are using chatbots for simple service queries, as this provides the user with information on low-priority cases quicker and improves perception of IT support. Chatbots are readily scalable and can be made easily accessible. It often makes sense for all users to engage with a chatbot in the first instance. The user answers questions about the issue and the chatbot assigns the next available and/or most suitable agent. IT support desks typically have information on tens or hundreds of thousands of cases, so it is viable to teach an AI chatbot how to respond to different situations. This is fine for non-critical cases, but there will always need to be an option for a user to raise a critical case and speak directly to a skilled service engineer. The chatbot could ask two or three simple questions to ascertain if the issue is critical and, if it is, reroute the case to a senior service engineer as a matter of urgency.

You may wonder what the implications for this are if you work in IT support. If your role is purely to triage cases and allocate ticket numbers, then your role is likely to be under threat. If you undertake basic diagnostics without much user support, then again your role may be under threat. However, if part of your role is to communicate directly with users, keeping them calm and guiding them through steps they may find tricky, then you will probably continue to do this.

What may change is your company's expectations of the number and complexity of cases you will complete. You will need to ensure you use the new AI tools to maximum benefit in managing your caseload. Maybe you could speak to a user, ask them to use an automated diagnostic agent while you do something else, and promise to call them back after a few minutes to discuss the results and next steps?

Deconstructing customer service

Now you have an insight into the thought process, let's consider a broader customer service or telesales role, such as a service centre for a bank account opening team. Let us look at a business opening an account at a traditional high street bank.

The applicant completes an online form and uploads supporting documentation, such as company registration information and the directors' identification documents. These are sent to a number of internal teams at the bank to undertake credit and criminal record checks, validate the business and decide what services can be offered (types of accounts, credit card and other facilities). Most of the major UK retail banks are constrained by legacy

IT infrastructure. Therefore, there are numerous manual data entry processes in this workflow.

A 'sales' agent then gets in touch with the customer to go through the application and ask questions about anything that isn't clear. The case is sent back to the internal teams, including credit risk allocation, who approve the account. This then passes to different teams who undertake the tasks necessary to open the account.

It is likely that a number of these roles will be automated by Robotic Process Automation bots; however, there is still a need to engage with the customer. Some of the most profitable customers for banks are those who have both their business and personal accounts with one bank. However, unless you have both a high level of personal wealth and a multi-million-pound business, you will need to be fortunate to have the bank treat your relationship with them holistically. I think this will change as the banks are missing out on a swathe of profitable customers.

What learnings can you glean if you work in a bank back office or sales role? Firstly, if you are purely back office doing data entry or basic decision making, your role may be at risk. You may want to position yourself as a point of escalation for the complex cases that aren't a clear 'accept' or 'decline'. If you are more at the front end and talk to customers about one aspect of the bank's services, then it is probably worth acquiring more knowledge of other services the bank offers. You could suggest to your boss that you could operate more flexibly as you will be able to discuss more products with customers. Alternatively, you could further develop your engagement management skills so you can be the prime point of contact for a customer.

Human attributes required

Continuing our move up the value chain we will now look at roles where more time is spent on unstructured interaction with customers and suppliers. These could involve negotiation of complex contracts, a customer service assistant in an upmarket or high-value goods retail outlet or someone responsible for customer experience at an event or restaurant. Often the people fulfilling these roles undertake both these bespoke tasks as well as more mundane ones.

Consider a purchasing officer for a large company. Their day-to-day work includes reviewing expenditure by supplier and product/service line, compiling reports for managers, preparing requirements documents by liaising with the folks who want to make a purchase, placing purchase orders and following up with suppliers for deliveries. In terms of time allocation, probably two-thirds of the time is allocated to the mundane work. Therefore, this role will change considerably as AI becomes more integral to their organisation.

I believe that the split of work between the mundane and the higher-value bespoke work is typically tilted towards the mundane for most of these types of roles. If this strikes a chord with you then my thoughts are: (i) that you should not resist the loss of the mundane and (ii) you should develop your skills to be better at the aspects of your role that require abstract thinking, emotional intelligence and critical thinking. These may be the commercial aspects of the role such as developing a proposal and/or negotiating a contract. If you are retail- or service-oriented then this could include establishing a rapport with the customer, guiding them to items they may be interested in or tailoring the service so it feels more personalised to them. You can also consider how you can add further value if you have more time as the mundane work has been reduced or eliminated.

I am an expert

Highly-trained people with a specialist skill or expertise have historically been highly valued by society. These roles cover a wide range, from people undertaking physical work that isn't repetitive and/or requires creativity, through to the professions: doctors, lawyers, accountants, architects, teachers, etc. These roles often carry an elevated status in society, albeit sometimes less apparent nowadays. I provided examples earlier in this chapter of how some aspects of these jobs were changing already. I think that over the next decade, we will see a more fundamental change, enabled by AI, in how these roles operate within the fabric of our society.

Skilled craftsmen

We have already seen skilled craftsman disappear from many factory lines. Nowadays it is usual for skilled human craftsmen to only undertake factory line work for bespoke manufacturers. An example is Rolls Royce, the prestige car manufacturer. Each car is designed to a bespoke customer specification; much of the leather and wood interior is still handcrafted at their factory in the south of England.

Even though skilled craftsmen no longer work on large factory lines, numerous small companies and sole traders design sculptures or wooden structures, for example staircases, to order based on a customer specification and agreed design.

If we break these roles down, we see that there is some bespoke, unpredictable work and some that can be automated. Taking a brief from the customer, developing, and evolving the design, all require human skills and are unlikely to be replaced. However, chiselling or casting the design is lower-value work. In the last century I would have argued that the dexterity of the skilled craftsman was very much a specialist skill. However, techniques such as 3D printing (particularly) bring a mechanised capability to build whatever the craftsman designed.

The role of the skilled craftsman continues to evolve, and I believe that AI will cause it to evolve further. Forty years ago, it involved talking to customers, roughing up a design drawing and then spending considerable time making the required object. Now it involves talking to customers, producing and refining mock-ups on a computer, selecting a suitable material and inputting the design specification into the 3D printer or other manufacturing device.

There are already AIs that create artistic pieces that can be turned into sculptures. This process needs guiding by artists. I believe that the use of AI to aid creative design will become more mainstream over the next few years. This means that AI will take on more of the work producing the mock-ups and selecting materials. Therefore the role of the skilled craftsman will move further up the value chain to: (i) glean a better understanding of what the customer has in their mind's eye when they commission a piece, (ii) guide the AI tools through the design process and (iii) engage empathetically with the customer.

The professions

Richard and Daniel Susskind undertook extensive research into the potential impact of technology on the following professions: accountants, lawyers, doctors, architects, journalists, management consultants, teachers and the clergy. They published their findings in the highly-esteemed book *The Future of the Professions*. Their considerations were far wider than purely the practical impact of AI. They reported that each profession had differing levels of enthusiasm for technology and that some had embraced the changes already. The point they make is that the professions will not be immune to change, not just because of AI or even technology, but because society's view of their value has altered over time.

For the purposes of this book, I will consider the change that could be enabled due to the proliferation of AI. This is in the context that knowledge is democratised, there are countless sources of knowledge, opinions interpreting events and texts available on the internet – many for free and some for modest fees. As discussed earlier, some maybe fake or erroneous, so it is necessary for you to hone your skills at correlating facts. The convenience of having this information at our fingertips probably exceeds the downsides. This means that the requirement for professionals to provide us with information is no longer a pre-requisite.

Remote services

Historically, many of the professions have sought to establish a trusted inter-personal relationship with their clients, pupils or congregation. Key to this has been face-to-face meetings and/or attendance at lessons or services.

There had been a slow drift towards these services being delivered remotely. Extracurricular courses are increasingly online, many religious services are streamed over the internet as well as being held in the place of worship, videoconferencing is slowly being adopted for meetings between doctors, lawyers and accountants and their clients/patients.

This trend has been accelerated by the need for people to be more remote due to the Covid-19 pandemic. Even though communications technologies are good, they do make it harder to establish a close inter-personal relationship. I don't think the public is as concerned as the professions themselves about this. Therefore, one of the challenges for the professions is to better personalise their service and differentiate themselves.

They also face new AI-enabled competitors. As an example, part of the role of teachers and the clergy is to provide counselling and pastoral services. Now, there are AI-enabled apps such as Headspace and Calm to help people reduce anxiety. There are apps providing pastoral services, although I am unaware of any using AI at the moment. I think it is only a matter of time before AI programs can enhance the services currently provided by these apps.

If there is an educational or pastoral part of your role, I urge you to think about how you could scale a more personalised service, perhaps using your skills to complement the AI enabled ones. There may be value in providing interpretation of laws, regulations or biblical texts; maybe in teaching skills to analyse life scenarios and apply religious or ethical business values to these learnings? I suggest you think about how you can realise value for your thoughts too. Most of all, I suggest you look at what AI can do to help you spend more time using your emotional intelligence and abstract and critical thinking skills.

Elimination of routine

Accountants and lawyers have historically spent hours going through detailed documents and accounts to collate the information they require either for a transaction or to complete an audit. Typically, their business model has been to have junior staff do this and charge the client an hourly rate. The market has applied cost pressure to this business model over the last 10–15 years; this has sometimes led to outsourcing the low-level work to lower-cost mass review centres.

Accountants have been more agile in developing new lines of business; they now offer a range of broader business advice than purely compiling accounts. They help clients with expenditure analysis, providing in-depth business insights and fraud detection. Accountants are embracing automation. The proliferation of cloud-based accounting packages such as Xero and QuickBooks has hastened this trend. AI has a role to play in reading the unstructured text, especially on invoices and purchase orders so they can automatically be loaded into the accounting systems; additionally it will facilitate greater automation of back-office processes.

If you work in this field then the opportunities are more likely to be in client engagement to manage delivery of a suite of services, structuring complex transactions and arrangements, and developing tax mitigation strategies.

The legal sector has been more conservative and embraced automation less enthusiastically than others. The typical business model of hourly rate charges suits the sector well and there is less of a commercial driver for change. However, over the last thirty years we have seen government services in many countries automate and become easier to use; this means that the necessity to retain a lawyer for many day-to-day transactions is becoming less necessary as you can fulfil them yourself.

Notwithstanding this conservatism, AI is making inroads, particularly in the US. Companies have been set up to process case law and align it to the judgments made in court. These AI systems can then be used to assess the likelihood of a positive outcome based on the facts pertaining to a case. AI systems are also being used to assist with workflow management, reviewing documents and compiling contracts. This means that legally trained folk need to focus their skills on client engagement and architecting transactions.

Health and wellbeing

Maybe you, like me, value very highly the expertise of healthcare professionals. We would probably find it deeply troubling to think that AI will replace them. I consider this unlikely: one of the greatest productivity challenges global society faces is the scalability of healthcare. This is born out of the expectation that healthcare can do so much for people and the frustration that it always seems to be constrained by resources, even in countries where budgets increase substantially. The other factor is the ever-rising demand placed on healthcare, predominantly due to the ageing populations in many countries.

Better and faster

The first concern when automating any clinical process is, will it work? In January 2020, Google Deep Mind published a paper in *Nature* about the use of AI for breast cancer screening. Their studies, in collaboration with UK- and US-based universities, concluded that AI delivered more accurate results than clinicians and there were fewer false positives and false negatives in both settings. Standard UK practice is for each scan to be reviewed by two clinicians;

the advantages of the AI over this double clinical review were less striking but still demonstrated greater accuracy than this double clinician review.

This does not mean that AI should be used to replace the clinicians, who have access to much more information, such as the patient's medical records and previous scans. This means they can make informed decisions not just about the cancer but also about the patient's overall medical situation. Please bear in mind that the study also indicated that in certain situations the clinicians were superior to the AI. From my reading of the learned comments, I believe that the way forward is to develop an operating model that uses AI working in conjunction with clinicians to deliver more accurate output, faster.

Proactive and streamlined

I mentioned earlier in this chapter the impact of the Covid-19 pandemic on working practices. One of the most striking changes in the UK has been the evolution of the NHS working practices. Email, online service and video consultations became mainstream within days or, at most, weeks. AI will do more than just streamline the delivery of services: it will reduce the routine work that clinicians and practitioners need to do. AI is capable of processing the vast volume of data that can be captured from a patient's biomarkers and supporting the delivery of proactive wellbeing and treatment regimes.

Patients in their own homes are often monitored through a series of blood tests and district nurse visits. Much of the time, there is no requirement for clinical intervention. The use of apps for patients to report how they feel and other remote monitoring tools (eg many heart pacemakers already link to a central monitoring service) enables interventions to be more targeted. The decision for human intervention is currently made by a human after something has gone wrong. In the future I envisage AI processing this data and providing a pre-emptive early warning so a proactive intervention can be made.

Throughout the healthcare system, medical staff spend much time writing up notes after seeing a patient. I recently spoke with a friend who is a paramedic in the UK. He said that after each call out, whether it is serious or not, they spend at least twenty minutes filling in forms. Much of the information on these forms is derived from readings taken from monitoring equipment; AI can enable the automatic completion of these forms.

Probably one of the most time-consuming aspects of medical care is triaging an initial patient query so that the patient receives the appropriate level of medical input. The consequences of misdiagnosis and missing something sinister are serious. Therefore, any triage solution needs to be alert to this.

In the UK, there are telephone helpline services, some staffed by clerks reading from a computer and some staffed by nurses or doctors. These are currently not sophisticated and frequently ask people to attend a hospital as a non-urgent case, which is often not the best course of action.

AI could bring more intelligence to this process over time. I don't believe that people will be replaced by computers, as it is necessary to have empathetic communication with the patient. However, basic symptom checking and data gathering could be undertaken by AI before the triage personnel engage with the patient to discuss further investigations and/or the treatment plan.

Making people better

I think it will be a long time before we see robots undertaking surgical procedures, if ever at all. We already have robotic-assisted surgery which is used in minimally invasive procedures. The surgeon manipulates controls and the robotic arms actually make the incisions. I discussed previously how AI is a powerful image-analysis tool. I envisage AI being used to help guide the surgeon by providing greater information about the images he or she is viewing. Again, this is an example of AI helping someone do an even better job than they are doing now, but certainly not replacing them.

I believe that AI can assist medics too. There are numerous drugs available that appear to perform similar jobs. However, selecting the right drug for a patient isn't easy. Some have side effects on patients with various conditions or allergies, some are contraindicated for patients that are already taking certain other drugs. Addressing this sort of multi-dimensional decision is what AI is particularly good at. I do envisage it being used as a decision-support tool by medics. Ultimately, it will not replace an experienced doctor who has seen many patients and the sometimes unexpected reactions they may have to various drugs.

My hope is that the health sector uses AI to remove much of the administrative burden from health professionals, aid their decision making on treatment plans and provide more early advice to patients. That way the clinicians, nurses and paramedics can spend more of their time doing what they signed up for – helping people!

Top of the tree

If you are sitting in a management role, you may be thinking how can I be replaced, my job is about leading people and making business judgment calls. To some extent I think you are right. I do think your job will change significantly, though.

If you run a department where the staff undertake routine work such as data entry or triaging initial customer service requests, you may find that there is an expectation that you do significantly more with less.

If you lead a team of experts providing services internally and maybe also to customers you may find that (i) there is greater demand from the expert members of your team for better tools to do the job and (ii) there is increased expectation on levels of productivity.

If you work at the front end of the business, eg marketing, product/service development and sales, the pace of change will continue to accelerate. I think that there will be more demands on you for perceptive and meaningful insight. I also think that your judgment calls will be more visible, especially regarding anticipation and realisation of future business. Understanding your customers and adjacent market sectors will be vitally important, as will the ability to adapt at pace and execute with precision.

If you are in management then I encourage you to get ahead of the game. You may find my simple mnemonic useful: just DIVE right in.

D is for Data

One of the learnings from the AI projects I have undertaken to date, is that many enterprises could realise the benefits AI has to offer much quicker, cost-effectively and safely if they approached the management of data as though it was a critical business asset. The key things that you can consider are:

What sources of trusted data do you have? Ideally these should be derived from the data you collect day in, day out while undertaking your business. This includes every engagement with a customer, however passive or unstructured. Please remember that AI is effective at processing unstructured data: emails, tweets, social media posts, videos and pictures. Therefore, as well as collating data about customer purchases, browsing history and other data with empirical values, collate everything they do with your brand, whether it is communication with or about your brand.

I encourage you to bring together teams of different people to work together creatively, to consider how this data could be used to derive insights that would be of business value. I would like you, and your team, to consider if the data your business collects is different from the data collected by your competitors, or if you can enhance this data set by adding other data to it – perhaps some from the publicly available sources such as government statistics, the FAANGs or other data organisations.

I is for Integrity

Using AI reflects on your personal brand as well as that of your company. As public awareness grows about AI, I expect the demands for reassurance to increase. I discuss the structural approach I recommend for organisations later in this chapter. The purpose of any initiative you develop to maintain the trust of your stakeholders is to be able to answer the following questions:

- Can you explain how the algorithm works?

- Can you defend the output?

- What will your customers, staff, suppliers, the general public and investors think?

- Can you demonstrate that the AI is operating within the law and in compliance with data regulations?

V is for Vision

I encourage you to look 3–5 years into the future. Consider how the role your team fulfils would change if (i) they had more time available as the routine aspects of their roles were undertaken by AI-enabled bots, (ii) the use of AI tools gave your team more information at their fingertips to help them do the higher-value, more human activities they undertake and (iii) you and your team were able to better personalise the services you deliver to your customers, whether internal to your organisation or external.

I recommend you then sketch out parts of the operating model, especially (i) the inputs your team need to do their new jobs, (ii) the outputs they will deliver and to whom and (iii) metrics to measure effectiveness and efficiency of the process and its output.

E is for Employees

You will be asking your team to go through a major transition which many will find difficult or even traumatic. It is unlikely that all the team will stay but you will want to maintain a happy, motivated culture. This will certainly challenge your change management capabilities. Once you have mapped out this future operating model, you can decide what skills will be required. This will be the basis of the change journey and development framework for your team members to acquire and develop these skills.

If you are currently in a management role, I believe that what you will be expected to do in terms of resource use, developing insight, delivering results and innovating will probably step up significantly.

Doing and using AI

AI will create jobs as an industry in its own right, but there will also be casualties. I discussed earlier in this chapter the types of roles most at risk. I also think that, as organisations embrace AI, you will see many job functions evolve rather than disappear altogether.

In the short term I see growth in demand for data analysts who can collaborate with businesspeople. They will need to define the types of insights that would help the business, and to assess the feasibility of developing a program to deliver them. Companies may need to consider recruiting new STEM graduates and/or how they upskill their current data analysts. For the latter there is much suitable self-help training available from the technology behemoths like Google, Amazon and Microsoft. This doesn't require the learner to have sophisticated technology skills – an appreciation of numeracy and a lively, enquiring mind are more important.

I mentioned earlier that data entry and data processing roles were at high risk. While much of this work may be outsourced, ethical companies that are sensitive to the perception of their brand may choose to work with outsourced providers to reskill them. It would be nice to think that companies have data in nicely organised databases and that all this data is labelled consistently. Sadly (or maybe happily in this context!), this is not the case. Once AI projects start there will be a need to split data sets for different parts of the project and to continually test the output to validate that it isn't biased or erroneous. These roles could be fulfilled by existing outsourced providers if they are prepared to reskill their staff.

You may feel uneasy about how all this data will be kept safely and legally, and rightly so! I see significant growth in the cybersecurity function, as well as in the number of people dealing with public requests for information about how their data is used and instructions on which data can be retained.

From a structural perspective I believe that companies should appoint a Chief Data Officer and a Chief Trust Officer as C-level roles. The former would be responsible for everything to do with data: keeping it secure, how it is stored and labelled, and ensuring that there are appropriate mechanisms in place to fulfil compliance and regulatory requirements. This will encompass many of the existing data management functions that are probably resident in the IT department. The Chief Data Officer will have responsibility and accountability for both regulatory compliance and data usability, with the goal of data being recognised as a key business asset. I believe that such a role will eliminate, or at least reduce, the interdepartmental squabbles regarding data use that I frequently had to mediate during my consultancy career.

As for the Chief Trust Officer, this is a new role that is extremely important in the AI era. As the general public becomes more aware of what AI is and how it works, it will need assurance that any AI programs are truly objective and fair in their outputs. As well as providing external oversight to the data compliance processes, the Trust Office needs to review all AI solutions and satisfy itself of their efficacy. The sort of questions they should be asking are:

- What is the output from this AI program and how will it be used?

    o What actions will be taken based on the output?

- How can stakeholders, including the public, ask questions and raise concerns about the solution?

    o Who will review these and what guidelines will they follow?

- What data is used to train the AI algorithm?

    o Where was it derived from?

    o How has it been anonymised?

    o How easily could an original data supplier be identified from the data?

- Could alternative patterns be identified by the AI algorithm because of the data?

    o How was the data labelled? By whom?

    o Could there be some unintended human bias?

    o What process is in place for sampling results and detecting unintended outcomes?

The assurance undertaken by the Chief Trust Officer should not be an afterthought: the need to trust AI should be embedded into the company culture if it is to be an integral component of the business's operating model.

Businesses spend significantly on HR departments to shape their workforces. If AI is to become another part of the business which makes decisions that affect people's engagement with the organisation, it is reasonable to expect companies to invest properly in building this capability too.

Organisations using AI will become more agile. Staff roles may change or at least be adjusted regularly; it will be important that staff can be trained quickly and cost effectively. Therefore, I anticipate expansion in the training and development functions. I expect many training courses will be through remote learning, typically by watching video tutorials. These will need to be produced, there will need to be 'experts' in each role who can provide more in-depth guidance and training on a specific aspect of a role someone finds difficult. Training will need to be much more dynamic in most organisations than it currently is.

In every company the needs will be slightly different. I have made generalisations to highlight the key trends and hopefully provide you with some insight into the types of mindset you will need in order to do well in your company rather than become a redundancy statistic.

CHAPTER 7:

Don't Get Left Behind

I make no apology for saying this again. Please don't think that all AI will do to your life is enable you to do what you do now, but quicker. I believe that it is going to transform the way we live and work during the 2020s.

AI will not change society on its own, though. There are other environmental, social, political and technology trends at work too.

Green

Probably top of mind is climate change. There have been political initiatives and summits for years. I think the factor adding more force to this imperative is the growing groundswell of opinion that things need to change. In the UK we are seeing more efforts to persuade or compel people to use public transport and/or cycle or walk more. This is particularly true in city centres: some cities, for example York, have announced plans to ban private cars at certain times. Other initiatives include using green technologies to power public transport: at the time of writing, over 30% of London buses are diesel-electric hybrids rather than just diesel, thus reducing emissions.

Less middle class

In the developed world we are seeing an erosion of the typical middle class: the rich are getting richer and the poor, poorer. This trend became more noticeable after the financial crisis in 2008. As the recovery took hold, most asset classes rose significantly in value and the jobs that were created were typically lower paid and less secure than many of those lost during the downturn. This has led to the development of the gig economy, where people do one or more jobs on an ad hoc basis for hourly payments and with little job security. Some people with highly valued skills have done very well as they can realise a high value in the market. However, for the majority this is bringing considerable stress and insecurity.

Allied to these divisions in society we have seen a trend towards more extreme political views. This has manifested itself in election victories for candidates who are prepared to disrupt the status quo. My expectation is that in many countries we will see more government policies to facilitate more inclusive societies. It is unclear what the financial cost will be. This leads us to consider the economic trends.

Money has no value

In the financial crisis of 2008, we saw governments bail out retail banks to an extraordinary extent. This use of taxpayer money has fuelled the increase in inequality. However, I believe what is even more telling is that we see a devaluation of money as the prime driver in the economy. There is discussion in more and more countries about providing a universal basic income.

Technology everywhere

Earlier in the book I discussed the creation of vast amounts of data through IoT, robotics and high-speed communications. There are also developments in healthcare, and a technology called blockchain that could be the basis of a future currency, which are discussed in more detail later.

Suffice it to say at this point that using these new technologies effectively will require intelligence. This intelligence can be human, but when it is artificial it will work quicker and more consistently. I mentioned previously that AI was being regarded as the fourth industrial revolution. I don't think AI will deliver on this promise in isolation, it will need the support of these other technologies.

I discussed these trends as I hope you will think about how you can benefit from AI over the next decade. You can't do this in isolation from the prevailing trends in society. Your journey will need you to navigate through the environment you live in as well as use AI. I don't for one minute think that AI will be a panacea for all of society's ills; what I do think is that it will deliver a significant increase in productivity, which can help us all improve society as a whole. Over the next few pages, I will outline my thoughts on what you can do to realise these opportunities.

Finding fulfilment

AI can help you reach towards your desired lifestyle. You may have a vision of what 'good' looks like for you. It could be a more rewarding role in a company, it could be self-employment, it could be more time to pursue a hobby or interest. Whatever it is, the key is to use AI to boost your personal productivity. That could be by reducing routine activities at home or work, or by augmenting you in some way, so you can use more effectively the time gained to do the things you enjoy.

In the work scenario this may be slightly easier as the workplace is often metrics-driven. Numbers are important in the workplace, but other factors are becoming important too – for example, employee engagement and wellbeing, and corporate social responsibility. I realise that you are probably compelled to achieve your work objectives. However, you may be able to add more value by transforming your role or suggesting and/or leading a new initiative in the social space.

Work-life balance is also important: you need to find time for hobbies and proper relaxation. Maybe you don't feel that you have time to pursue a hobby as seriously as you would like. Perhaps you want to run a marathon but can't find the six to eight hours per week to train; perhaps you want to research your family history, religious background or take up a creative activity in the arts as a hobby. The key is to make the time without compromising things you have to do like work or looking after children. I urge you to review your daily routines and actively consider how AI can help you eliminate the repetitive, unfulfilling activities, whether they are at work or home.

Day in, day out

Let me give you an example: if you have an active social life, meeting colleagues and friends for drinks or snacks after work, have you ever thought about how much time and effort goes into finding a date and venue? Extrapolate this to work, where finding slots in diaries seems to be a never-ending task.

Imagine having a calendar bot. It could collate all meeting requests you send and receive. Once a day you could go through these and advise how you want to meet the person (eg drinks, dinner, in-person, video call), when you want to meet the person (weekday evening, specific times) or times to avoid, etc. The bot then checks travel time between physical meetings, the availability of others and makes the required reservations.

There are already calendar bots available, for example x.ai, that can deliver some of this vision. I think it is reasonable to anticipate that x.ai or others will deliver increasingly intelligent capabilities over the next few years. I am advocating a productivity journey. If you are coming on this journey, then you could start to think about how you organise your schedule and how you can do that more efficiently. There will be barriers, especially social ones. I have friends of my age who still prefer a phone call to make an arrangement. Social factors will slow adoption but, as with many technological advances, people do adopt them in the end.

How much time do you spend on jobs at home? I fully expect robots to be developed to relieve some of this routine. A Japanese company recently demonstrated a robot that tidies up a children's toys in a playroom. This is a finished product but had yet to be launched into the market with a price tag at the time of writing. You can already purchase robotic vacuum cleaners and lawnmowers from Amazon. These devices may not yet be fully autonomous, but I suspect they will shortly.

Removing routine from our lives will not happen overnight; not just because the tools aren't available or cost effective but because we all get some level of satisfaction from the feeling that we are doing stuff. This will take a mindset change. I think it is worth embarking on the journey as

I feel sure that you will have many unique human skills, emotional intelligence, critical thinking, abstract thinking and creativity that you would like to use more.

Record and analyse

Earlier in the book I discussed the importance of gathering data. Whatever you have decided you want to spend more time on, start to think about what information would be useful to gather. The objective is for you to be better at the things you choose to do; it could be spending more time playing golf, it could be another hobby, it could be work initiatives. Whatever it is, start to gather information that could be useful to teach you how to do things better in the future.

Taking the golf example – there are already apps claiming to use AI to analyse a golf swing. For instance, SwingAI has created a 'swing index' that is derived from 21 aspects of a player's golf swing. Users record a video of a golf swing and get instant feedback on where they can improve. If sport isn't your thing, there are experimental AI apps that generate art from photos and music so, if you prefer being creative, there will be options for you too.

When you know what you want to do, type that into Google followed by the letters 'AI' – you may be surprised that there are already AI tools available to help you! Whether or not you choose to use these apps, I recommend you investigate the data they gather and use. Once you know this, you can start to store this type of data. At the time you do choose to use AI, having historic data may well help. Please remember that the data can be text, numbers, videos, audio tracks or images.

Turning to work productivity, you are probably more aware of data that exists in your workplace. However, have you considered using the unstructured data, such as email content and marketing documents? These contain data that is unlabelled. If you run a sales team you may decide to see if there is a correlation between the content of a letter accompanying a quote and the success of the quote. If you are in customer services, is there a correlation between the content of emails sent from customer service representatives and the satisfaction scores given by customers? These are the sort of questions AI will be able to help you answer. Whatever role you have at work, think about data you generate and information you use. You are seeking insights that would help you do your job better or quicker.

Mindset

Let me give you an example of the thinking that will thrive as AI takes root. Imagine you work in a control and surveillance centre for a city's municipal authority. You probably have access to CCTV cameras for security and road traffic management.

Your responses are typically reactive: either (i) you see an event and follow it on CCTV while alerting the front-line responders, or (ii) you receive a radio message from a shop security guard that a theft has occurred and they provide a description of the perpetrator. You then look through the

CCTV screens and use the nearest cameras to try and pick up the suspect so you can direct the front-line responders to the incident. The success of the response may be limited, as it is reactive. If the incident was more serious, for example including violence, then the consequences could be far worse than pure financial loss.

Therefore, you think about what 'good' or, at least, 'better' would look like. It could possibly be a proactive determination of risks and deployment of resources prior to an incident. You sit back and consider the data that you have available to you:

1. CCTV footage from shops

2. CCTV footage of road, pavements (sidewalks) and pedestrian-only areas

3. Radio and/or automated alerts for incidents

4. Incident reports

5. Public transport usage information

6. Traffic congestion information

7. Car park utilisation

You develop in your mind a concept which runs as follows: there will be various circumstances that precede an incident – for example, one or more vehicles following the same route round the city centre repetitively or a group of people gathering around someone begging on the street.

You then look for tools that could detect such scenarios, and evaluate whether the information you have could provide the leading indicators you need. You also review historic records to confirm that there will be value in detecting these incidents proactively. The reason I selected this scenario is that AI is already good at image analysis and used widely for security applications. I therefore expect the outcome of your feasibility assessment to be positive. You will then seek funding for your initiative and define an implementation schedule.

I know that the real world isn't as straightforward, especially in organisations that are subject to budgetary constraints and/or competing demands for funding. The points I wanted to highlight were the visionary and data aspects of the thought processes needed to create incremental value rather than just focussing on cost saving.

Always keep learning

You may associate the word productivity with cost cutting and efficiency. I used to think like that, until I realised just how important proactive continual learning is. I had always adapted to change well and had a disruptive streak, but didn't take much time to structure my learning – I just absorbed my experiences and learned in my own way. Over the last decade I have found that it is more important to structure my learning and be proactive in changing, rather than reactive. The world is changing faster and faster; AI will accelerate this pace of change regardless of whether you decide to proactively engage with it or not!

This doesn't necessarily mean you have to study on structured courses; after all, with the internet we all have access to knowledge. What it does mean is that the perspectives or insights you provide will be valued more and more, especially if they are actionable in some way. At the basic level, to fuel your thinking, you need access to relevant content. This is potentially tedious and time consuming. There are AI-powered tools to help with this – I already mentioned inflo.ai. There are others that actively search a large body of content for relevant material. Iris.ai is designed for scientists and can sift through large volumes of research papers to seek out the relevant material.

At the time of writing I see that these tools are mainly designed for marketing-content creation or scientific research. However, I believe that a wider range of applications will be developed as the technical barriers are overcome.

AI is being used more and more by academic institutes to generate more relevant content and provide more personalised support, while keeping course costs competitive. I think this is still in its infancy but there are more and more applications of AI being used in coaching and to identify relevant content for people.

I believe that the people who feel most fulfilled will be those who use AI tools to reduce the routine in their lives and assist them with on-going learning – not only courses but also coaching and identification of relevant material to read or view.

CHAPTER 8:

Side Hustles Become Easier

One of the recurring themes I have discussed is that AI industrialises things we could do, but don't have the time or resources to do, due to the scale or complexity of the problem. This means it can help us to do things quickly and easily that have not been regularly done previously.

There are more AI tools available every week that can help you; I mentioned before that it is always worth doing a web search adding 'AI' to the end of what you are looking for. The FAANGs provide a range of AI computation services and tools on a subscription, or pay-as-you-use basis, so you do not need to worry about the computational aspects. They also work with the communities they attract to compile open source collections of data that can be used to help develop AIs; it is possible to use these as a core building block of your side hustle.

As the tools are available, the most important thing you need is the idea. I have looked at numerous small lifestyle AI businesses, and some commercial ones that grew from lifestyle businesses. I see a recurring theme: many were founded because of an individual's passion to develop a solution for a problem they saw in society.

It's your business

One of the key aspects of any business is to be differentiated. AI will not do that for you. I discussed earlier how AI cannot replace our most human capabilities, emotional intelligence, abstract thinking, creativity and critical thinking. Your side hustle must use your unique human skills to personalise a service, product, or brand.

I think it is worth unpacking this a little more. You may be helping people who at best will feel insecure with a transition they are making. More likely, especially if it is a relationship, health, or lifestyle transition, possibly with significant financial implications, your prospective client may be feeling anxious and depressed.

Deciding what problem your venture solves for people requires a level of empathy that you may only feel having lived through a similar transition in your own life. Even if your service offers a business solution, the success of your venture will often be determined by how you can appeal to your customers' emotions and secure their trust.

Delivering the service requires acute emotional intelligence. Your prospective customers may not be in a good place, or at least will feel something is missing in their lives. Even if they aren't distressed, they will want to feel that they have achieved what they expected thanks to your product or service, and that the time and money they invested were well spent.

Unique insight

I hope that this book may prompt you to ask questions of yourself, or even me. I think the hardest question you could possibly ask me is, "What would be a good business idea for me?". While I understand many of the small businesses I see quite quickly, there are some that stick in my mind as taking me a while to get my head around. Typically, these are businesses where (i) the founder has a unique insight into a market need that I don't have and (ii) the founder is passionate about this market need.

While I can't give you a direct answer, I think I can give you some pointers on where to focus your thoughts if you want to develop a side hustle using AI. I see four key areas to consider when developing an idea:

1. You have a passion for something based on your life or business experiences. You feel deeply that you have something you must share.

2. If you have expertise in something, can you apply this in a unique way that makes it easier for customers to consume? Alternatively, can you apply this unique expertise to do something that hasn't been done before?

3. Do you see a problem that you have a unique way of solving?

4. Perhaps you have a creative concept (fashion, art, music) and want to create a following.

Delivering the service

Once you know what you want to do, you need a vision of how you will deliver the service. Maybe through one-on-one coaching, an online course, videos, podcasts broadcast on YouTube or iTunes, or webinars. If it's a product, then you need fulfilment routes. You may also wish to create a community of interest around that product.

Whatever it is, I think it is likely that AI can help. This may be by analysing customer data, by getting you more information and insight from publicly available material or by filtering customer enquiries. It may even be as simple as using AI tools to save you time during the day, so you have more time and energy to pursue your interest and figure out how to monetise it.

Testing the market

Having decided what problem you will solve, you will need to test the market to see whether there is a demand and the service would be valued. Traditional surveys securing structured data are one approach. However, these often only provide a superficial response, as people provide the answers that they think you may wish to hear. It is much better to engage in discussion, maybe through community groups or by creating discussion threads on social media. If you do pose questions, then these should be open, so they encourage people to speak freely. These responses can provide a more in-depth insight into the problem you are planning to address.

AI is extremely helpful at analysing unstructured data; it is often used to provide companies with sentiment analysis based on their Twitter conversations. You should capture all the threads and feedback from these discussions so they can be further analysed using AI tools. This will provide much helpful feedback as it conveys human feelings as well as needs.

It will be necessary to identify and attract suitable customers. Social media advertising facilitates advertising to targeted groups. You may prefer blogging and establishing an online community to gather a following from which to select your customers. Again, in a similar way to the validation of the problem, you can use AI tools to analyse these conversations and find the right hooks for a more targeted sales approach.

Refinement

Having zoomed in on the problem you wish to solve, it is necessary to refine your offering and delivery model. If this is one-to-one and face-to-face, then there is probably limited use for AI. However, if it is more remote, either by being online or one-to-many, then AI may have a role to play.

I mentioned previously face recognition tools that could be used to determine levels of attention and engagement. I can see the day, not too long in the future, when online courses become intelligent. The pace and level of explanation provided from the course material is based on an AI monitoring system that assesses how readily the trainee is assimilating information.

It's AI, so you need data!

This isn't as terrible as it sounds – there is so much data available nowadays. Look at the number of online, non-paywalled publications. Look at the number of videos on YouTube. Look at data you observe on social media.

There has been a growth in the concept of open source data. There are numerous sites available from governments, UN-backed organisations, academia, big tech companies and individual contributors.

The UK and US governments publish all sorts of data about society. The UK government's open data website makes it clear that this data is available to people to build products and services; could this be your start in journalism, analysing trends in society?

If you are serious about using AI for a side hustle, then please do visit Kaggle. This is a repository for data, facilitates collaboration on data sets and often runs competitions. Winning a Kaggle competition can give the credibility needed to enter a new market. Google is also worth a visit: it hosts datasets including images, text, phrases, books and other publicly available information. It also encourages the use of this data as a playground for developing new insights.

This list isn't exhaustive; the point is that there is information everywhere for you to use. Visiting these sites will give you an idea of the possibilities.

Let's get creative

People love experiences that they feel are personalised or help them partake in something exclusive. Some people dread going to a gala dinner and finding someone has the same outfit they have. Designer brands come and go, some large, some quite niche, but they have a value. Many people are prepared to pay a premium for basic food and drinks if they have an upscale aura associated with them. Consider Starbucks, they can charge much more for a cup of coffee than a local café!

The Google Magenta project provides tools and aids for both artists and musicians. Music generation is typically done based on a selection of genre and mood.

A commercially available leader in this field is AIVA, who provides the opportunity to develop bespoke music for video games, background music and a more personalised tune to reflect one's mood or personality.

Cross and Freckle is a New York-based T-shirt manufacturer. It superimposes images from Google's Quick Draw image database on to T-shirts that retail for $25 each. The images were designed by AI based on the doodles of 15 million contributors who played a game on its site.

As well as product design, AI will boost the options for selecting clothing combinations that go together and for providing styling services. Some clothes retailers have already entered this space. For example, Stich Fix, a US company that entered the UK market last year, uses data that it collects on customer preferences, to tell its team of personal stylists which clothes to send out to customers. I can't help but feel that there will be opportunities for independent stylists to use similar AI algorithms to identify clothing combinations for their customers. These could be based on clothes they like that they see in pictures and items available from retailers. Alternatively, AI could potentially be used to make bespoke designs and create the patterns for them to be manufactured.

Munchies

Personalised food experiences are becoming more and more popular. For a while now you have been able to go into your local coffee shop and select the type of milk you have in your coffee, any additional flavours and even how hot it is. One of the ways Burger King has differentiated itself from McDonald's is by saying you can have the Burger King Whopper just the way you like it. While McDonald's has allowed customers who order at the till to personalise their selection, they have only recently put customisation fully into the hands of the customer at the self-ordering points.

AI takes this a step further: apps are being developed to predict taste preferences and major manufacturers are using AI to help them develop products. McCormick Corporation, the food flavouring and colouring manufacturer, and IBM are collaborating to use AI to predict flavour combinations. Gastrograph is an app that is designed to aid food producers in developing the appropriate flavour for their target market. The technology is still evolving but I expect it to become mainstream over the next three to five years and create opportunities for food entrepreneurs.

Aesthetics

The opportunities AI presents for art are rather more nuanced. It can take pictures and adjust them. For example, researchers at the University of Tübingen in Germany have created depart.io, which can take video frames or pictures and turn them into a piece of art in a style that you choose. This can then be used to make a wall-hung picture or added to a clothing item.

The options for using AI to develop creative side hustles, especially in music and fashion are endless. If you have a market or can create a community then the side hustle can focus on that and use commercially available tools to deliver the product.

Sport: playing, coaching, reporting

Sport is a component in most of our lives, whether that is as a participant, coach, reporter, supporter or an opinionated spectator in the pub or your front room. Few (if any) of us are professionals, but most of us want to do better when we participate or understand more when we report or spectate.

Up until a couple of years ago, detailed analysis was only available to professional teams who track players through wearable technology such as GPS trackers to measure performance, or accelerometers to measure impact and thus proactively mitigate injury concerns. AI and video analytics are enabling many more options for professional teams to develop their tactics and training plans. AI-powered video analytics is scaling into the semi-professional and serious amateur sectors too.

The current market leader is an Israeli company, PlaySight. They use these techniques to provide analysis on over thirty sports. These range from team sports such as football (soccer), rugby and basketball to individual sports such as martial arts and swimming.

As video recordings of most sports are readily available, and this £600m sector is expected to grow fivefold over the next few years, I expect more companies to enter the market. The quality and relevance of the analytics should improve, and the cost should fall. Cricket Australia works with an Australian AI company, Gameface, to analyse tactics and individual performances of its cricket team. Gameface also offers solutions for football (soccer) on a commercial basis.

Two guys in their twenties made the rugby news headlines in England earlier this year. Both have played rugby at an average level (by their own admission) and have other jobs. They are now an important part of the England manager's strategy team: Gordon Hamilton-Fairley and James Tozer are using AI to identify the critical tactics required to dominate key areas of the game and exploit opposition vulnerabilities.

If video analysis is a step too far, AI can still help. In the UK we have an annual fair for young scientists and engineers. At last year's Big Bang Fair, a semi-professional football team, Wingate and Finchley FC, demonstrated their AI football coach, which had been commissioned for development by the Big Bang Fair. The AI coach analyses basic data about the club's players and the opposition team's preferred formation and style of play. The AI coach then recommends a starting formation and style of play as well as some tactics, such as substitutions, during the game.

It is your choice whether you use AI to improve your own performance or to provide valuable insights to generate income. It may be that you can use it for both, especially if you enrich the data. Let me give a purely speculative example. You may compete in cycle races at the weekends. Maybe there would be value if you could combine your race data with data on your diet and training regime in the previous week. The insight from this may help you improve your performance; if it does, could you monetise these learnings as a coach?

Have fun

Whatever your side hustle is, I think it is most important for you to ensure you find it fun and worthwhile. AI can augment your natural talent by providing advanced insight into the data you will gather and by removing some of the drudgery from the day-to-day aspects of running a business.

It will be you, though, not any AI tools, who make or break the business so you should also keep your skills and knowledge at the forefront of your chosen market niche. Guess what, there's an AI tool for that!

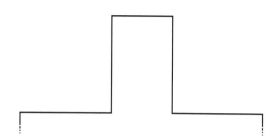

PART 4

THE
FUTURE
YOU

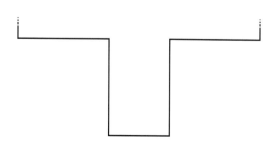

CHAPTER 9:

AI Will Transform the Way We Live

Society is changing anyway

I hope that you appreciate that AI will be one of the technologies that fundamentally changes the way we live; I hope you share my view that it will be the fourth industrial revolution. How it changes the way we socialise, work and play will depend on other factors. Not just other technology developments, but also global societal attitudes.

Moving around

I believe that one of the learnings from the first twenty years of this decade is that globalisation has caused trends in the way we live to spread internationally very quickly. Urbanisation and consumerism are global phenomena.

I mentioned urbanisation and consumerism. A consequence of this has been much greater use of transportation. This includes people travelling to work, either in their own cars or on public transport services, people travelling overseas by air for business or holiday, and goods being shipped globally by air or sea. Many transport hubs and city streets are perpetually congested. The levels of pollution from all these fossil fuel-burning engines is colossal.

One response to urbanisation has been a rise in public transport solutions. There are faster, bigger trains for mass transit between urban areas and metro rails, bus networks and last-mile solutions, such as on-demand bikes and scooters, within these areas. We are starting to see fewer polluting vehicles and more electric vehicles. The development of driverless vehicles continues at pace. I think that soon we will reach the point where usage considerations will be the gating factor on the adoption of driverless vehicles. The blockers I see are (i) how a driverless vehicle will respond to avoid an accident, especially if a collision would cause human injury and (ii) determining liability if there is an accident between a driverless and driven vehicle.

Therefore, I think that we will see sections of city centres and holiday resorts where only driverless vehicles are allowed, probably with a low speed limit. I expect many of these to be provided as an on-demand service where users rent them by the hour or even less time. It may also be viable to have convoys of driverless trucks on main haulage routes, especially in countries with a large land mass.

I know people in California who today use the driverless functions on their Tesla cars to drive on the motorway and perform intricate manoeuvres such as parallel parking. Currently, human attendance is still required in case something unexpected happens – unexpected events are typically caused by humans!

I haven't mentioned drones, but I think there is little doubt they will proliferate, especially for deliveries of small number/weight items. Clearly, there will need to be regulations and safeguards developed for their use; these may limit their areas of operation but that remains to be seen.

Paying your way

I mentioned earlier how I felt money had become devalued after the 2008 financial crisis. I think that this was in fact the acceleration of a broader trend. Since the 1970s, countries have relaxed ties between their currencies and gold holdings; this has ultimately led to the ability for countries to 'print money'. One consequence has been growth in the availability of credit and a reduction in the use of 'cash'. Money has become an entry in a database rather than holding an item of intrinsic value. I think we will see a decline in traditional banking as a one-stop-shop for money.

There are already numerous companies offering current account and internet payment services through apps; these are cheaper and more convenient than using traditional banking services. There has been a rise in peer-to-peer lending through apps.

Some countries, eg Israel, are beginning to embrace cryptocurrencies, such as Bitcoin, through regulation. As the regulation develops, I anticipate more stability in the exchange range between cryptocurrencies and the existing currencies; the cryptocurrencies will also become more acceptable as the tax authorities find it easier to work with them. Therefore, I expect us to see greater adoption of cryptocurrencies by the general public, especially as their value should not be linked to the economic environment in a particular country. This means that, as a matter of course, people could carry two or more currencies in their electronic wallet.

As well as cryptocurrencies, there are other technology developments that will influence how AI is used over the next decade.

Data everywhere

Data is food and drink for AI. It isn't just the increased use of social media and the internet that gives this data. I have already mentioned the Internet of Things (IoT). So many devices transmit data: if you use Google Home or Alexa, then every voice command is sent and stored by Google or Amazon respectively. If you have a heating or security system controlled from your phone, then these commands are probably stored somewhere. One of the better-known home security systems is Ring. Ring is now owned by Amazon, so information from the cameras and doorbells will be stored along with your searches, purchases and everything else you do using Alexa, Kindle or their stores.

IoT will continue to grow. It seems that virtually every device we own now connects to the internet. This data will be fuel for the growth of AI.

The other technology you have probably heard about is 5G. It will enable more accessibility to very fast internet and communication services. AI enables virtual reality and computer vision applications; 5G will help get these applications into your hands wherever you may be.

Understanding us

An extension of these themes is the development of wearables. Over the last few years the major smartphone manufacturers have developed intelligent watches. As well as telling the time and being fashionable, these watches can act as fitness trackers, record key biomarkers such as heart rate and provide entertainment and location services.

I expect you will see 'intelligent clothes' before the end of the decade. Perhaps they will change colour and be programmable, so you can have them change to reflect your mood? Already there are products marketed that record additional biomarkers such as ECG and breathing rate. These are applicable for sports performance and care of the elderly. It isn't hard to see how the opportunities in this market could expand and the types of data that could be collected.

The final area of technology I want to address is genomics. Genomics research is important, as it is the science behind disease prevention and improved health. It is a complex, multi-disciplinary field that will progress anyway. I believe that AI processing of the data that already exists and is being captured every day will accelerate positive developments significantly.

Health and wellbeing

One of the biggest global societal challenges is mass health diagnostics. Often tests and procedures exist but the gating factor is getting the tests done and receiving the results. Being able to pay can help but often, for the more complex conditions, there is still a significant wait.

Many diagnoses require visual examination of a sample or a scan by an experienced clinician to identify if there is a problem. This is particularly true for cancer diagnosis, which I mentioned in Chapter 6. As it is so important not to miss potential problems, there are often processes that require more than one clinician to undertake the analysis. AI has been shown to be more effective than a single clinician at identifying various types of cancer and other issues. However, confidence is not at a level where it would be acceptable to have diagnosis undertaken by AI alone.

Rather than a definitive yes/no answer, AI provides a level of certainty that, say, cancer cells are or are not present in a sample. This information can then be used to determine how many clinicians review the sample to check. This still represents a significant streamlining of the process. Training AIs to undertake diagnosis for all conditions will take many years; I think that we have reached the point where this process of training AIs can start. I believe that we can have a good level of confidence that we will obtain some useful AI tools over the next few years.

Chronic conditions

The use of non-invasive techniques, such as wearable technology and smartphone apps, can facilitate the initial screen for a chronic condition. The data can be gathered at the patient's convenience or in accordance with a schedule agreed with the clinician. AI would be able to analyse this data, along with other medical data about the patient, such as current medications, and provide an initial diagnosis. This would save a trip to the doctor's surgery for examination. I expect we will see an increase of video consultations with family doctors and more non-invasive gathering of data to replace the examination in the doctor's surgery.

This gathering of data can extend to visual signs too: earlier in the book I mentioned BlueSkeye, who are using AI processing on a facial imaging app to assess mental health. I expect that the collection and synthesis of data by AI will lead to proactive diagnosis of conditions, especially neurological and mental ones.

Fighting diseases

Humankind's efforts to combat disease are global but not completely coordinated. This isn't necessarily a bad thing, as the competition between research institutions and drug companies probably spurs innovation. Developing new drugs takes many years and requires considerable safety and efficacy testing. It is much easier if a combination of existing drugs can be used to treat a new disease, or if an existing vaccine can be adapted to prevent people catching a new disease or strain of a disease. To do either of these requires sifting through countless research papers, clinical trial reports and drug usage advisories. Considering different combinations of drugs is a complex task. AI will help narrow down these considerations so that experienced researchers can spend more of their time assessing potential solutions rather than investigating approaches which may or may not work.

Tracking apps and mobile phone data are already being deployed to assess and help reduce the spread of a disease. These potentially compromise people's privacy. Many governments, especially those in the West, provide reassurance that the data is mostly anonymised. However, if in the future governments and the FAANGs shared more data, for example the personal profile data that the FAANGs acquire, then AI could be used to identify potential spread of the disease based on contacts and also lifestyle. I think we will see backlashes from time to time against AI. If governments use personal profile data to predict future behaviour on an industrial scale, this may be a step too far for many citizens.

Robotics is already being shown to aid rehabilitation and help the physically disabled, especially when the disability is caused by a neurological event such as a stroke. China and Japan are two world leaders in his field. This application is at advanced stages of research but has yet to be fully commercialised. There are plenty of options, including remote exoskeleton units to aid movement, localised devices to aid movement on a specific limb or even robots to show patients the exercise they need to do and assess their performance.

I can see these techniques being extrapolated to the wider population for rehabilitation after a major limb repair, and for care of the elderly to help them get back on their feet after a protracted hospital stay.

Getting active

The final part of this journey from illness or injury to wellness is the ability to be active and participate in physical activities. Sports and recreational activities continue to evolve to increase participation – just look at the development of the Paralympics over the last twenty years. I discussed in Chapter 7 how AI can help you improve your sporting performance or experience. AI can even create new sports!

As a proof of concept, you may wish to look up Speedgate. This is an AI-created sport that was derived from rugby, soccer and croquet by AKQA, a global innovation and digital communications company. Speedgate is defined in detail with rules, equipment specifications and even videos of the game.

You may be familiar with virtual reality; it has been used in an entertainment setting for a while. It is starting to be used as a training aid for top-level sport. Virtual and augmented reality were around before AI became more mainstream. AI augments these technologies as it enables object tracking and a greater level of interaction between the virtual environment and your actions.

STRIVR is a company with its origins in the Stanford College Football Team. Their technology creates such a level of reality that it is now used as a training aid in the NFL. It is particularly useful for teaching players how to react to high-pressure situations. The benefits are that there is no need for other players to be involved when coaching individual skills; consequently the risk of training-ground injuries is reduced. Trent Edwards, who spent seven years as quarterback in the NFL after playing college football at Stanford, makes for compelling listening. He discusses how STRIVR's technology is used as a training aid for NFL quarterbacks – this is a position where they need to play the ball, in a chaotic scenario, before being slammed to the ground.

I think we will see VR tools become available to help coach individual skills in team sports, such as passing a rugby ball or football (soccer ball) under pressure, batting in cricket and specific skills in which top-level players are seeking that extra edge.

I believe that developments in the AI field will enable virtual reality (VR) and augmented reality (AR) to be major enablers of change over the next few years. I will discuss that further in the next section about communication and engagement.

Communications and engagement

AI isn't a communication and media technology in its own right. What it does is enhance our use of existing technologies such as video conferencing, digital marketing, personal assistants (Alexa, Google Assistant, Siri and Cortana) and virtual reality. AI is also an enabling technology for robotics.

The services you receive and the way you go about your day-to-day activities will be more personalised. You will have the option of running many of your household tasks from your smartphone or by using voice commands. The information presented to you, be it news articles, weather and transport updates or advertising, will be based on preferences you have shown in the past. As most routine communications will be electronic rather than paper, you will be able to have your inbox dynamically sorted so the top priority matters are brought to your attention.

Your digital personal assistant will organise your calendar. Over time, I think it will become more and more helpful. It will learn to predict your preferences for venues and times to meet with different groups of friends. You will be able to engage with friends better through video conferencing tools. You will be able to access augmented reality features so you can better share experiences without having to travel and meet.

Recently students were unable to travel to their graduation ceremonies at the Business Breakthrough University in Tokyo. The University secured a fleet of human-size robots from ANA holdings. The robots wore graduation gowns and hats. The students controlled their robot from home. Their face was on a tablet so they could see the Dean and interact with him. Maybe in the future, some pubs and coffee bars will have a fleet of robots available that customers can hire by the hour if they are unable to join friends at the physical location to meet up?

I expect that in the future you will be able to have more control over your work-life balance, especially if you can work from home more often. You will be able to engage with work colleagues using technology more than you can now. This engagement will be more realistic as augmented reality techniques are applied.

Over the last decade both Cisco and Microsoft have demonstrated techniques to transmit 3D images of people to other locations. This greatly enhances the reality of the engagement. Microsoft calls this 'holoportation' and are continuing to develop the technology so that it will be able to operate over normal high-speed wifi connections of 30Mbps to 50Mbps.

Whether or not holoportation catches on, I still think that AI will make our remote business engagements less vanilla. I discussed earlier the use of sentiment analysis to determine how a call centre agent was affecting the feelings of the person they were speaking with. I expect these sentiment analysis techniques to be extended further, maybe even to give real-time feedback on video conferences on the emotional response of others. Imagine if, when you were talking, you could see the outline of the other people's faces change from green to red if you said something controversial!

I know that Google glasses weren't favourably received in the past. Perhaps in the future we could all wear glasses (or even contact lenses) with head-up displays that give us insight into other people's sentiments? I believe AI will make this technically possible, though I am unsure how it would be accepted by the general public.

Learning and development

I see significant growth in learning and development courses, both specific to a work environment and to leisure and personal development. An increasing number of these will be through remote learning. The use of virtual and augmented reality, possibly coupled with robotics, could extend the scope of these online courses to the physical world. Could you see a time when machine maintenance is learned through remote virtual or augmented reality techniques?

AI could enable personalised pacing and selection of course content for individuals; it could also enable greater interaction to create a more engaging experience. Courses could include an AI coach to answer questions and monitor levels of engagement with different parts of the course. The AI coach could suggest extra content for aspects of the course the learner is interested in or content in an alternative format, for example video rather than text, for aspects of the course that the learner is having difficulty engaging with.

I think that the 2020s will be the decade when remote engagement finally becomes the norm in society. There are societal drivers for change which have become more prevalent as the millennials and Generation Z have started to influence behaviour in our society. Inclusion, reducing carbon emissions and work-life balance are top of mind. There is also the compelling event of the coronavirus pandemic. This has forced a reformatting of everyone's life. The technology is available to support the required transitions. It will become even more economically viable over the next few years and AI will provide the intelligence to make it effective and usable.

The future of work

In Chapter 6 I outlined my thinking on how jobs would evolve and mentioned some jobs I envisage disappearing. In Chapter 2, I hope that you gleaned insight into the attributes that people who are successful in the AI era are likely to exhibit. Using these parameters as context I will share with you some ideas on new roles that may be created in the future. The list is far from exhaustive; it is presented to give some ideas of the lateral thinking that should be applied to realise the opportunities AI can offer.

I am also assuming that anyone who has read this far is committed to the journey of self-development and on-going learning that I believe will typify the stand-out people of the next decade.

Customer engagement exemplar

A fundamental aspect of any business is customer engagement. There has been a trend of this changing from transactional to more relationship-based. Just consider a car purchase – it used to just be a question of doing a deal and driving the car off the forecourt.

Nowadays, the major car brands wish to engage with you before you have even made a decision to purchase a car, they want to find out about your usage patterns and gain insight into requirements you may have. Then, when you go to the dealership, they are keen to have face-to-face discussions. If you want finance, this can mean a long wait as most dealers don't have many regulated finance sales staff. The car dealer is then dependent on retaining your interest and commitment over a protracted sales cycle.

As it is now possible to finance cars using third parties, customers may organise the car finance separately, which erodes the dealer's margin and also deprives the car manufacturer of any opportunity to set resale values at the end of the finance term.

Let's think how this operating model could change over the next few years. The pre-sale customer engagement can be more personalised. The sales process can start earlier by offering a customer a video call and maybe a video tour of the vehicle they are interested in. There could be augmented reality options to simulate the experience of riding in the car – maybe not the movement, but at least the noise and visual effect, possibly both as a passenger and a driver.

When the customer is enticed into the dealership for a physical test drive, the salesman could organise for them to meet the finance specialist who might be based in a call centre but would appear in the dealership as a robot with them on a screen. The finance package could be tailored based on your anticipated driving style, which means it would be more cost effective for you and the residual value ascribed to the car would be more realistic for the dealer. A service specialist could also see you, possibly also as a robot fronting a remote expert, to propose a personally tailored service package.

The implications are that the salesperson will need to interpret much more data and be able to establish a longer-term trusting relationship with the customer. Additionally, there would be a number of new expert roles, such as experts in the driving experience, experts in tailoring the service package, etc.

Brands, not people, will have a relationship with you

I think that these relationship-based multi-modal engagements will become the norm. The relationship will be between the customer and the brand rather than an individual. This means that the style of engagement can be adapted so it meets the customer preference. If you have a routine enquiry such as when your next service is due, you are best served by a chatbot that can answer immediately; if it is a more complex issue, it is better that you are routed quickly to a relevant expert.

There is currently an industry forming around customer journeys and customer experience; more and more companies are setting up customer success functions in their service operations. I believe that as AI takes root, the end-to-end customer journey and experience will be considered holistically. I think that by the end of this decade it will be a whole business function of its own, rather than split between the marketing, sales and service departments.

The changing face of IT

I anticipate similar adaptations to the roles in IT departments. Even the most conservative organisations are starting to realise the benefits of cloud-based services ranging from data centres provided by Google, Amazon and Microsoft to fully functional Customer Relationship Management (CRM) systems such as Salesforce, and service-ticket management systems such as ServiceNow.

The role of IT therefore needs to adapt: the IT imperatives of organisations will increasingly shift towards structuring data assets and cybersecurity rather than running their own infrastructures. This will be an evolution, so I do not expect the traditional IT roles to disappear completely. However, the better-paid roles will probably be those that can work with business clients to glean preceptive insight from data. People who organise and secure that data will also be highly valued.

You may ask what happens to the current outsourcing industry that undertakes so many routine IT tasks? I expect that many organisations will find that their data assets are inconsistently labelled. Therefore, I think that these IT outsourcers may find opportunities in labelling data and even developing software routines to validate data. I also see a whole raft of testing opportunities as routine testing of the AI output will be required to ensure the lack of bias in the AI algorithms.

In the same way that jobs will adapt and be created, so will different industries adapt and new opportunities emerge.

AI will become a major industry in its own right. While there will be roles requiring great technology skills, I anticipate that many of the roles will require capabilities to glean or provide insight. That may be insight from data, or insight into an industry or market. The availability of tools and programs such as Alexa Skills and Microsoft's AI partner program will help organisations develop professional practices and service businesses based on these foundational technologies. I expect many new, skilled roles to be created in this supply chain.

AI is also a technology enabler

Earlier in this chapter you read about other technology developments. None of these operate in a vacuum; my feeling is that AI will be the glue that accelerates the usefulness and adoption of these technologies. As such, AI will lead to the creation of jobs in other industries too. A good example is driverless vehicles: AI effectively gives the driverless car its eyes, ears, and other monitoring systems. Similarly, the ability of drones to identify and track a target location or person, in the military scenario, is enabled by AI.

Medical technology and telemedicine will change the social care sector. For example, I think we will see companion robots for the elderly, helping them to organise their medications and keeping an eye on their wellbeing within agreed privacy parameters. These companions may also provide access to entertainment options and possibly social groups from within someone's own home. Think of the job and business opportunities here. I see these creating a market far larger than the current social care market.

Drones

While drone usage is currently limited, there is significant potential there too. Drones could be used for day-to-day deliveries of medicines and goods. Amazon has been working on this idea for a few years. I think that this will ultimately become a safe and secure delivery method. A whole new industry to regulate safety and control congestion will be required.

Data privacy and monetisation

Looking more at individual level, one recurring theme is data privacy. Ultimately, how much information about yourself are you prepared to see go to unknown providers? Do you think that at some time in the future you may want to monetise this information? When these questions become uppermost in the minds of many in the population there could be a market for new services. How about a data broker who assembles a sample data set that you create and secures bids for it?

How about if in the future there is a data privacy service that (i) ensures you have ticked the appropriate boxes on web-based services and mobile apps to keep your data private and (ii) routinely makes subject access requests on your behalf to ascertain what data is stored by whom and then, if a price isn't agreed, asks them to delete it. This is just one idea, possibly fanciful, but there will be others.

A day in the life

On Tuesday evening you check your wellbeing monitor. It suggests you should try and get 8 hours' sleep as you had a heavy session at the gym earlier in the day. You go to bed at 10.00pm and use the relaxation app, that is especially trained on your bio-markers, to help you go to sleep. Your alarm wakes you at 6.30am. The water heater in your apartment had been alerted by your home control system, which was notified by your early morning alarm to turn on at 5.30am, so you had sufficient hot water for a shower. After you get up, the kettle boils water and the robotic arm makes you a cup of coffee. While you are getting dressed you ask Alexa about the weather for the day and the time of the shuttle bus to the station.

On your journey you review the selected news items in your feed. As you have a busy day ahead you choose to listen to these while checking your calendar and notes for each meeting that have been collated by your (automated) personal assistant.

Your day starts with a physical meeting with your team. You then dial into a video conference with your customer. During the call you receive several alerts that the customer is feeling anxious and that these are most acute when you discuss the commercial aspects of the proposal. Consequently, you change tack during the conversation and instead of continuing to present you ask more open questions. These help you understand that the customer wanted a different structure for the proposal, so you agree to rework it and book another meeting.

Your friend Julie asked you to meet with her and her colleague Sam over lunch. Julie was keen to hold the meeting in a restaurant as she wanted to discuss a potential side hustle with you and him. The restaurant is 45 minutes' travel away. They have robots you can hire so you can be present at the meeting. You receive the login details for the robot and join Julie and Sam at the bar for an informal drink. You then head over to the table with them and eat your packed lunch while they tuck into their quinoa salads. The session is interesting, so you all agree an in-person follow-up within a week or two.

Your next meeting is the trust committee for the recruitment system the construction company you work for uses. You noticed that job applicants from a certain area of London were not receiving the same proportion of job offers as others in the capital. You are going to request further investigation, as this neighbourhood has demographic, housing and crime profiles typical for the inner suburbs where most of your workers come from. It therefore seems odd that there is an anomaly in the number of successful candidates from this area. You need to present your findings and agree an action plan with the data insight team and the algorithm testing team. You need to identify whether there is a problem with the AI-based recruitment system.

The meeting is via video conference. It is particularly useful. You and your colleagues identify that for the area of London in question, the data used to develop the algorithm was much older than that used for other locations. It all seems to make sense. The area in question was regenerated 10 years ago. The historic data didn't represent the demographic profile of the current residents. A plan is agreed to use more current data to train the algorithm and fix the issue. A couple of people are assigned to check any cases that have been processed by the old algorithm. You agree to raise these concerns with the local community engagement team and to work out a communication plan.

You head home early to have supper with your partner and two young children. After supper you help get your children ready for bed while the robot clears up their toys.

After the children are in bed, you and your partner play a virtual reality game of badminton. You then attend a video conference with colleagues in New York to discuss the lessons learned from the faulty algorithm. You read a little, check your wellbeing monitor and head off to bed.

Your choice

If you let your mind wander forward 5 or 10 years and think about the capabilities enabled by AI, you may well think of many other ideas than those mentioned in this book. I really hope you do! My objective in writing this book is to stimulate you to think about your future, outline some ideas to get your thinking started and to offer frameworks for developing them.

I sincerely hope that you can find time to pursue your vision and that at least one of these ideas works out for you.

USEFUL LINKS

Alexa and Amazon

Alexa Introduction
https://www.alexa.com/

Alexa Skills Store
Type into search and click on the URL

Amazon Personalize and Other AI Services
https://aws.amazon.com/personalize/

Anxiety and Sentiment Analysis

audEERING
https://www.audeering.com/

BlueSkeye AI
https://BlueSkeye.com/

Cogito
https://www.cogitocorp.com/

Headspace
https://www.headspace.com/

PainChek
https://painchek.com/uk/

Creativity and Food

Cross and Freckle
https://thistshirtcompanydoesnotexist.com/

Dapart.io
https://deepart.io/

Gastrograph
https://www.gastrograph.com/

Magenta Project
https://magenta.tensorflow.org/

Databases and Competitions

Kaggle
https://www.kaggle.com/

UK data records
https://data.gov.uk/

US data records
https://www.data.gov/

Google

Google AI Homepage
https://ai.google/

Immersive Learning

American Football and More
https://www.strivr.com/

Microsoft

Microsoft AI Tools
https://www.microsoft.com/en-us/ai/ai-platform

Productivity Tools

Content Production
https://inflo.ai/

Calendar
https://x.ai/

Robotics

Humanoid Robot
https://softbankrobotics.com/us/pepper

Warehouse Robot
https://www.owrobotics.co.uk/

Sports

Cricket and Football (Soccer)
http://gameface.ai/

Golf
https://swingai.golf/

Speedgate
https://playspeedgate.org/

Transportation

Aviation
https://aurora-ai.com/

ABOUT THE AUTHOR

John is an expert in the practical aspects of using AI and an experienced business consultant.

He is an active angel investor and board advisor for early-stage AI companies. John was the founding shareholder of Aurora, which became the market leader in AI solutions for the air sector, before a successful exit.

John led his own consultancy business for over fourteen years. He had the privilege to lead some of the most complex and challenging global business change programmes in the Telecoms, Technology and Banking sectors.

John has had the ultimate portfolio career: as well as working in his own companies he has worked for global organisations and SMEs in a range of roles including sales, business development, commercial and operations.

Following the sale of Aurora, John is pursuing his passion for the application of leading-edge technology to solve some of society's and business's 'hard problems'.

John can be contacted at:

Email: john@collaborative-ai.com

LinkedIn: https://www.linkedin.com/in/john-michaelis/

Twitter: JohnMichaelis@JohnMichaelis10